PUBLIC TELEVISION

Members of the Commission

JAMES B. CONANT
Former President
Harvard University

LEE A. DuBRIDGE
President
California Institute of Technology

RALPH ELLISON
Author

JOHN S. HAYES
United States Ambassador to
Switzerland

DAVID D. HENRY
President
University of Illinois

OVETA CULP HOBBY
Chairman of the Board
Houston Post Company

J. C. KELLAM
President
Texas Broadcasting Corporation

EDWIN H. LAND
President
Polaroid Corporation

JOSEPH H. McCONNELL
President
Reynolds Metals Company

FRANKLIN PATTERSON
President
Hampshire College

TERRY SANFORD
Former Governor of North Carolina

ROBERT SAUDEK
Robert Saudek Associates, Inc.

RUDOLF SERKIN
Concert Pianist

LEONARD WOODCOCK
Vice President
United Automobile Workers of America

JAMES R. KILLIAN, JR., *Chairman*
Chairman of the Corporation
Massachusetts Institute of Technology

HYMAN H. GOLDIN
Executive Secretary

STEPHEN WHITE
Assistant to the Chairman

GREGORY G. HARNEY
Staff Associate

JOAN CUMMINGS SOLOMON
Staff Associate

THE CARNEGIE COMMISSION ON EDUCATIONAL TELEVISION

public
television

A PROGRAM FOR ACTION

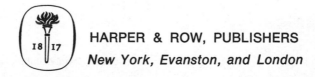

HARPER & ROW, PUBLISHERS
New York, Evanston, and London

Contents

Supplementary Papers

Preface

This Report of the Carnegie Commission on Educational Television is addressed to the American people.

The Commission has been sponsored by the Carnegie Corporation of New York, and its study financed by that foundation. The Commission was asked to "conduct a broadly conceived study of noncommercial television" and to "focus its attention principally, although not exclusively, on community-owned channels and their services to the general public. . . . The Commission will recommend lines along which noncommercial television stations might most usefully develop during the years ahead."

It was made clear to the Commission from the outset that within the general framework of its charge from the Carnegie Corporation it was free to set its own terms of reference and to operate wholly under its own direction. The Commission reports, therefore, as an independent group, solely responsible for its conclusions and recommendations.

In a letter endorsing the general objectives of the Commission, President Lyndon B. Johnson wrote: "From our beginnings as a nation we have recognized that our security depends upon the enlightenment of our people; that our freedom depends on the communication of many ideas through many channels. I believe that educational television has an important future in the United States and throughout the world. . . . I look forward with great interest to the judgments which this Commission will offer."

The stimulus for the formation of the Commission was provided in December 1964 at a conference convened by the National Association of Educational Broadcasters in cooperation with the United States Office of Education. At that conference, Mr. Ralph Lowell of Boston, after discussion with his associates at the Lowell Institute Cooperative Broadcasting Council, proposed the establishment of a commission to study the financial needs of educational television and the manner in which they might be met; a formal proposal for the establishment of such a commission was then drawn up by Mr. Lowell and Mr. C. Scott Fletcher of the National Association of Educational Broadcasters. The interest of John W. Gardner, then President of the Carnegie Corporation and now Secretary of Health, Education, and Welfare, was immediately engaged, and his efforts, together with those of Alan Pifer, then Vice President and now Acting President of the Carnegie Corporation, led to the creation of the Commission.

Throughout the course of our inquiry we have called upon many persons for their guidance and help; not once were we refused. No door was closed to the Commission's questions. A sense of importance and urgency was expressed by those who made contributions to our work. We can only conclude that there exists a widespread conviction that the tasks set before the Commission are widely viewed as of high priority.

During the year in which the Commission was intensively engaged in its study, eight formal meetings of the Commission were held, occupying a total of twenty-eight days. Smaller groups of Commissioners met from time to time between meetings, and consultations between the staff and members of the Commission were frequent. A high degree of commitment on the part of all its members was apparent to the Commission from the beginning to the end of the study.

Altogether, more than two hundred and twenty-five individuals and organizations have expressed themselves to the Commission, either by appearance before the Commission and its staff or in writing. Members of the Commission, its staff, or its correspondents have visited, in all, ninety-two educational television stations in thirty-five states, as well as the television systems of seven foreign countries. Those visits, and in particular the visits conducted within the United States, have provided for the Commission a body of information on educational television which is unique in both its scope and its quality.

We have conducted statistical surveys with the unstinting cooperation of all the educational television stations and state educational television commissions. We have been assisted by memoranda, articles, and studies from many sources, notably the growing literature on educational television.

During the summer of 1966, a conference was held at Endicott House in Dedham, Massachusetts, attended by thirty representatives of educational television, commercial television, and allied fields. Discussions on manpower, programming, financing, and instructional television were conducted by the conference.

An extensive study of model cost and system structures for educational television and Public Television was conducted on behalf of the Commission by Arthur D. Little, Inc., and proved very helpful to the Commission in the preparation of the cost estimates which will be found in the Report.

Some of the papers prepared for the consideration of the Commission and which appear to be of general interest or to have reference value are presented in the supplement to this Report. The Commission's own Report, which, in the final volume, precedes those papers, expresses views and conclusions that are sometimes in accord and sometimes at variance with those of the authors of the papers. Our Report is based entirely upon our own judgments and our own conclusions, which were often assisted but at no time determined by material prepared by others.

Our work has been ably supported at every stage by a devoted staff: Dr. Hyman H. Goldin, Executive Secretary; Mr. Stephen White, Assistant to the Chairman; Mr. Gregory G. Harney; Mr. Edward Weeks; and Mrs. Joan Cummings Solomon — all have given themselves unsparingly throughout the Commission's existence. We also appreciate the assistance of Mrs. Marcia C. Mather, Mrs. Maxine B. Oldenburg, Miss Frances Crawford, Miss Jane Sauer, and Miss Ruth Smith.

Both the Commission and the staff received invaluable assistance and counsel from consultants to the Commission. Because of their sustained participation, we note with special gratitude the professional services of Professor Sidney Alexander, economist; Dr. Mark Harris, author and teacher; Professor Albert G. Hill, physicist; Mr. Ernest W. Jennes, legal counsel; Mr. Donald C. MacLellan, physicist; and Mr. Charles Theodore, electronics engineer. In preparing its Report for publication, the Commission has been assisted and advised by Mr. Thomas R. Carskadon, Mr. Osgood Nichols, and Mr. John E. Woodman, Jr. We also note with gratitude the assistance of Mr. Arthur Singer, Executive Associate, the Carnegie Corporation of New York, who helped organize the study and served as its liaison with the Carnegie Corporation.

A complete listing of all persons and organizations that have contributed to the preparation of this Report will be found elsewhere in these pages. To all of them we express our deep indebtedness.

Upon his full-time assumption of the presidency of Hampshire College on June 1, 1966, Dr. Franklin Patterson relinquished his duties as Staff Director, but fortunately has continued as a member of the Commission. His responsibilities as Director were assumed by Dr. Goldin.

Mr. John S. Hayes resigned as a member of the Commission on October 1, 1966, after his appointment as Ambassador to Switzerland. His participation was extremely valuable. He was with the Commission long enough to have helped shape its principal conclusions and recommendations. We are happy that he joins all the other Commissioners in signing this Report.

The members of the Commission count it a privilege to have shared in this study.

JAMES B. CONANT	EDWIN H. LAND
LEE A. DUBRIDGE	JOSEPH H. MCCONNELL*
RALPH ELLISON	FRANKLIN PATTERSON
JOHN S. HAYES	TERRY SANFORD
DAVID D. HENRY	ROBERT SAUDEK
OVETA CULP HOBBY	RUDOLF SERKIN
J. C. KELLAM	LEONARD WOODCOCK

JAMES R. KILLIAN, JR.
Chairman

*See statement by Mr. McConnell on page 72.

Introductory Note: What Public Television Is

The system of noncommercial television in the United States has come to be known as educational television. This system includes (a) more than 120 stations which are owned and operated by educational institutions or other nonprofit educational organizations and which carry no advertising; and (b) National Educational Television (NET) a non-profit organization which provides most of the more ambitious programming and with which most of the stations are affiliated.

The Commission has separated educational television programming into two parts: (1) instructional television, directed at students in the classroom or otherwise in the general context of formal education, and (2) what we shall call Public Television, which is directed at the general community.

All television, commercial television included, provides news, entertainment, and instruction; all television teaches about places, people, animals, politics, crime, science. Yet the differences are clear. *Commercial television* seeks to capture the large audience; it relies mainly upon the desire to relax and to be entertained. *Instructional television* lies at the opposite end of the scale; it calls upon the instinct to work, build, learn, and improve, and asks the viewer to take on responsibilities in return for a later reward. *Public Television*, to which the Commission has devoted its major attention, includes all that is of human interest and importance which is not at the moment appropriate or available for support by advertising, and which is not arranged for formal instruction.

A Proposal to Extend and Strengthen Educational Television: A Summary of the Commission's Report

The Carnegie Commission on Educational Television has reached the conclusion that a well-financed and well-directed educational television system, substantially larger and far more pervasive and effective than that which now exists in the United States, must be brought into being if the full needs of the American public are to be served. This is the central conclusion of the Commission and all of its recommendations are designed accordingly.

Although our Report deals primarily with what the Commission has chosen to call Public Television rather than with instructional television, we believe it to be urgently in the public interest that both categories be extended and strengthened. We concentrate on Public Television in the conviction that this service both requires and is ready for immediate action. Instructional television, which we consider no less significant, needs intensive further study in the total context of the educational enterprise, and is the subject of a major recommendation to this end.

The programs we conceive to be the essence of Public Television are in general not economic for commercial sponsorship, are not designed for the classroom, and are directed at audiences ranging from the tens of thousands to the occasional tens of millions. No such system now exists to serve us as model, and hence we have been obliged to develop a suitable new arrangement to bring this kind of television to the country. The Commission's proposal deals primarily with that new arrangement.

Although it provides for immediate assistance to existing stations, this is a proposal not for small adjustments or patchwork changes, but for a comprehensive system that will ultimately bring Public Television to all the people of the United States: a system that in its totality will become a new and fundamental institution in American culture.

This institution is different from any now in existence. It is not the educational television that we now know; it is not patterned after the commercial system or the British system or the Japanese system. In the course of our study, we examined all those and others: members of the staff visited Canada, England, Italy, Germany, and Sweden, and papers were commissioned on the Japanese and Russian systems. We found in many countries serious and skillful attempts to provide superior television programming, and in some countries highly successful attempts. But when such a system was successful it met the special needs of society in terms of that society's culture and tradition, and there was little or nothing we could expect to import. We propose an indigenous American system arising out of our own traditions and responsive to our own needs.

Accordingly, the Commission submits the following recommendations for the consideration of the people of the United States, their government, and those who for two decades have created and sustained the various institutions that constitute educational television.

THE COMMISSION URGES IMMEDIATE ACTION TO EXTEND AND STRENGTHEN EDUCATIONAL TELEVISION

1

Page 33°

We recommend concerted efforts at the federal, state, and local levels to improve the facilities and to provide for the adequate support of the individual educational television stations and to increase their number.

An effective national educational television system must consist in its very essence of vigorous and independent local stations, adequate in number and well equipped. They should reach all parts of the country. They should be in-

° Page numbers in italics refer to full discussions of each recommendation in Chapter Three.

dividually responsive to the needs of the local communities and collectively strong enough to meet the needs of a national audience. Each must be a product of local initiative and local support.

Many good stations exist; they must be made better. Weak stations must be provided with the kind of support which will cure and not perpetuate their weakness. All educational television stations require greatly increased resources.

THE COMMISSION PROPOSES A NEW INSTITUTION FOR PUBLIC TELEVISION

2

Page 36

We recommend that Congress act promptly to authorize and to establish a federally chartered, nonprofit, nongovernmental corporation, to be known as the "Corporation for Public Television." The Corporation should be empowered to receive and disburse governmental and private funds in order to extend and improve Public Television programming. The Commission considers the creation of the Corporation fundamental to its proposal and would be most reluctant to recommend the other parts of its plan unless the corporate entity is brought into being.

The Corporation will exist to serve the local station but will neither operate it nor control it. Its primary mission will be to extend and improve Public Television programming. Programs financed by the Corporation will be made available to all stations, but each station will decide whether and when it will use the program. We stress the critical importance of having private funds available to the Corporation; such funds should be available at the outset.

3

Page 42

We recommend that the Corporation support at least two national production centers, and that it be free to contract

with independent producers to prepare Public Television programs for educational television stations.

One center now in being is National Educational Television, which should at once be strengthened.

4

Page 46

We recommend that the Corporation support, by appropriate grants and contracts, the production of Public Television programs by local stations for more-than-local use.

The greatest practical diversity of program production sources is essential to the health of the system. Stations exist which now produce programs of interest outside their own areas, but which are in need of further financial assistance. Other stations should be encouraged to develop comparable talent and capacity.

5

Page 49

We recommend that the Corporation on appropriate occasions help support local programming by local stations.

These would be low-cost programs prepared to meet the direct needs of the local community.

6

Page 53

We recommend that the Corporation provide the educational television system as expeditiously as possible with facilities for live interconnection by conventional means, and that it be enabled to benefit from advances in technology as domestic communications satellites are brought into being. The Commission further recommends that Congress act to permit the granting of preferential rates for educational television for the use of interconnection facilities, or to permit their free use, to the extent that this may not be possible under existing law.

The Corporation has the responsibility for the distribution of programs. Public Television can never be a national enterprise until effective interconnection has been provided both in order to distribute programs to educational television stations promptly and economically and to provide for live regional or national broadcasts when the occasion demands. The interconnection of stations should make the best of each community available to all communities.

7

Page 59

We recommend that the Corporation encourage and support research and development leading to the improvement of programming and program production.

Public Television should be free to experiment and should sponsor research centers where persons of high talent can engage in experimentation. The kind of experimentation once sponsored by the Ford Foundation TV–Radio Workshop is an example of what we are reaching for.

8

Page 61

We recommend that the Corporation support technical experimentation designed to improve the present television technology.

Intensive research and development could make possible significant improvements in picture quality or savings in frequency spectrum.

9

Page 66

We recommend that the Corporation undertake to provide means by which technical, artistic, and specialized personnel may be recruited and trained.

The Corporation should sponsor fellowship programs designed to attract talented persons into in-service training programs and into its research centers. In addition, it should provide stipends for senior fellows — men and women of

talent and experience — to enable them to spend periods
of residence at the various centers.

THE COMMISSION PROPOSES ENLARGED FEDERAL SUPPORT
FOR PUBLIC TELEVISION

10

Page 68

**We recommend that Congress provide the federal funds re-
quired by the Corporation through a manufacturer's excise
tax on television sets (beginning at 2 percent and rising to
a ceiling of 5 percent). The revenues should be made available to the Corporation through a trust fund.**

In this manner a stable source of financial support would
be assured. We would free the Corporation to the highest
degree from the annual governmental budgeting and appropriations procedures: the goal we seek is an instrument
for the free communication of ideas in a free society.

The excise tax will provide the Corporation with approximately $40 million of federal funds during its first year
of operation, rising gradually to a level of $100 million a
year. We propose that the rate be raised to 3 percent,
bringing in $60 million, after the first year. The Commission
intends these revenues to be added to those available from
other federal, local, and private sources to be used primarily
for the support of programming for Public Television. We
recommend that federal agencies continue to make grants
to educational television stations for special purposes.

11

Page 74

**We recommend new legislation to enable the Department
of Health, Education, and Welfare to provide adequate
facilities for stations now in existence, to assist in increasing
the number of stations to achieve nationwide coverage, to
help support the basic operations of all stations, and to enlarge the support of instructional television programming.**

The Commission views the responsibility of the Department of Health, Education, and Welfare as that of providing the basic facilities and operating funds for a national system of educational television stations. The Corporation, in contrast, will direct its attention to programming and related activities delineated in previous recommendations which are aimed to provide a new kind of Public Television for national and local audiences. The responsibility for instructional television for formal classroom use does not lie within the purview of the Corporation, but rather with state and local educational systems and the Department of Health, Education, and Welfare. The Commission urges, as an interim measure, extension and amplification of the Educational Television Facilities Act of 1962, which has been of critical assistance in expanding educational television.

THE COMMISSION PROPOSES CONTINUING STUDY TO IMPROVE INSTRUCTIONAL TELEVISION

12
Page 80
We recommend that federal, state, local, and private educational agencies sponsor extensive and innovative studies intended to develop better insights into the use of television in formal and informal education.

The Commission believes that the Public Television system it proposes will benefit the content of instructional television. But the Commission also believes that instructional television must be studied in the full context of education, and that further major investments in instructional television must benefit from the discovery of ways in which television can best contribute to the educational process. In addition to universities, nonprofit corporations, and the stations themselves, some of the Regional Educational Laboratories contemplated in Title IV of the Elementary and Secondary Education Act of 1965 might be appropriate agencies to conduct the necessary programs of research and development.

CHAPTER ONE
The Opportunity

Television has been fashioned into a miraculous instrument. The opportunity is at hand to turn the instrument to the best uses of American society, and to make it of new and increased service to the general public.

The Opportunity

Noncommercial television should address itself
to the ideal of excellence, not the idea of acceptability — which is what keeps commercial
television from climbing the staircase. I think
television should be the visual counterpart of
the literary essay, should arouse our dreams,
satisfy our hunger for beauty, take us on jour-
neys, enable us to participate in events, present great drama and music, explore the sea
and the sky and the woods and the hills. It
should be our Lyceum, our Chautauqua, our
Minsky's, and our Camelot. It should restate
and clarify the social dilemma and the political
pickle. Once in a while it does, and you get
a quick glimpse of its potential.

— E. B. WHITE, *in a letter to the Commission*

The object of the study undertaken by the Carnegie
Commission on Educational Television has been to assist
in the improvement of noncommercial television. As we
have proceeded in our task, we have come to see it in far
broader terms. We have become aware of television as a
technology of immense power, growing steadily more powerful. What confronts our society is the obligation to bring
that technology into the full service of man, so that its
power to move image and sound is consistently coupled
with a power to move mind and spirit. Television should
enable us not only to see and hear more vividly, but to
understand more deeply.

We have come to see that since the technology of television lends itself readily to uses that increase the pressure
toward uniformity, there must be created means of resist-
ing that pressure, and of enlisting television in the service
of diversity. We recognize that commercial television is
obliged for the most part to search for the uniformities

within the general public, and to apply its skills to satisfy the uniformities it has found. Somehow we must seek out the diversities as well, and meet them, too, with the full body of skills necessary for their satisfaction.

America is geographically diverse, ethnically diverse, widely diverse in its interests. American society has been proud to be open and pluralistic, repeatedly enriched by the tides of immigration and the flow of social thought. Our varying regions, our varying religious and national and racial groups, our varying needs and social and intellectual interests are the fabric of the American tradition.

Television should serve more fully both the mass audience and the many separate audiences that constitute in their aggregate our American society. There are those who are concerned with matters of local interest. There are those who would wish to look to television for special subject matter, such as new plays, new science, sports not now televised commercially, music, the making of a public servant, and so on almost without limit. There are hundreds of activities people are interested in enjoying, or learning about, or teaching other people. We have been impressed by how much we might have from television that is not now available.

To all audiences should be brought the best energies, the best resources, the best talents — to the audience of fifty million, the audience of ten million, the audience of a few hundred thousand. Until excellence and diversity have been joined, we do not make the best use of our miraculous instrument.

The utilization of a great technology for great purposes, the appeal to excellence in the service of diversity — these finally became the concepts that gave shape to the work of the Commission. In the deepest sense, these are the objectives of our recommendations.

Television and Education

In carrying out its charge, the Commission from the very beginning was troubled by the name "educational television." Justifiably or not, it sounds forbidding to many.

It calls to mind the schoolroom and the lecture hall. It frightens away from educational channels many of those who might enjoy them most.

Yet the great power of television, commercial as well as noncommercial, is that it continues to educate us long after we have left the classroom. It replenishes our store of information, stimulates our perceptions, challenges our standards, and affects our judgment. In the sum of what it presents, it is profoundly educative as life itself is educative, and perhaps all the more so because there is no formal syllabus to which we can refer so that we may see what we have learned.

Education is not always somber or laborious. It is coextensive with the full range of human experience and includes joy and gaiety as well as hard intellectual endeavor. Educational television should be no less. Education, in the true sense of the word, helps us derive progressively greater satisfaction from our work and from our play; educational television should be at hand to assist in the process.

Whatever the connotations that may for the moment be attached to the name, educational television is exactly the subject with which the Commission meant to deal. To abandon the term would have been in some sense to compromise with our own respect for the powers of education. The system we propose, then, is proposed as a system of educational television. We do feel the importance of distinguishing between its two parts — Public Television, directed toward the general public, and instructional television, dealing primarily with formal instruction. In making this distinction, however, we look upon these two parts as constituting a single whole.

Commercial Television

The Commission did not inquire closely into commercial television. Yet commercial television is involved. We believe that an energetic and well-supported educational television system will inevitably affect American tastes and American standards. Appealing to diverse audiences, it will reveal new realms into which, as they are developed, commercial television with all its impressive capabilities will be eager to penetrate.

We do not regard educational television and commercial television as distinct activities, each pursuing its own exclusive way. We deplore any inference that educational television cannot entertain as it addresses itself to its many audiences, just as we deplore any inference that commercial television should decrease its efforts to provide excellent programs of cultural and public affairs for the mass audience.

Station Visits

During the course of its study, the Commission was in direct touch with all 124 educational television stations then in operation, and sought within the time available to arrange staff visits to as many of them as possible. In the end, 92 stations were visited, and an extensive confidential report on each was made available to us.

The single theme in those reports that most impresses us is that of opportunity unrealized. From station to station the lament rises: so much that might be done, so much that needs doing, so receptive the small audience that is now reached, so little the resources with which to operate. The energies that are latent within educational television are immeasurable. The men and women who have committed their careers to educational television, and whose rewards have never been commensurate with their efforts, have lost none of their devotion and have managed to maintain their enthusiasm. Only the means are missing.

Their audiences are almost always small. Yet from the stations come reports, often transmitted with a sense of astonishment, that the audience is also broad. It is not limited to an intellectual or a cultural elite. If the members of the audience have anything in common, it is that they are a hungry audience, looking to educational television for something they do not find in their everyday lives. For many, it is also something they cannot afford unless it comes to them free on educational television.

The Unheard

The station reports reveal a programming pattern that is common to very nearly all the stations. It scarcely suggests the horizons toward which those stations, with adequate resources, might reach. In the large cities and the universities that possess educational stations, there is creative talent that has never found its way to television. There are performers of high professional skill who do not seek or would not necessarily meet the taste of the commercial mass audience. The man who might bring enjoyment to only a few thousand people should not be denied the opportunity to do so.

There is the whole living, meaningful world of civic affairs at something less than the national level. The educational stations have not had the funds or the physical facilities to deal properly with their own immediate environment. The cities have long since become a hundredfold too large for town meetings, but part of what the town meeting accomplished is certainly within the reach of educational television. And the matter is all the more important in an era when cities are suddenly confronted with an unending series of new problems that cannot be met by administrative arrangements alone: problems that demand the engagement of each individual citizen, who must be both informed and moved to act.

In the universities there are the scientists and the students of our society and of the societies with which we deal. They can be brought to recognize television as a medium that commands their attention. Public Television, elevating its own sights and those of its public, can help provide for the university a resource not unlike the university press, making its own contribution in terms it can freely honor. It is not merely a matter of calling upon the scholar for an account of his accomplishments, but of making for him a place within television to which he can repair as he is accustomed to turn to the printing press.

A Civilized Voice

As we have pursued our study, all that has come before

us strengthens our conviction that the American people have a great instrument within their grasp which they can turn to great purposes. Through the diversified uses of television, Americans will know themselves, their communities, and their world in richer ways. They will gain a fuller awareness of the wonder and the variety of the arts, the sciences, scholarship, and craftsmanship, and of the many roads along which the products of man's mind and man's hands can be encountered.

Public Television is capable of becoming the clearest expression of American diversity, and of excellence within diversity. Wisely supported, as we conclude it must be, it will respect the old and the new alike, neither lunging at the present nor worshipping the past. It will seek vitality in well-established forms and in modern experiment. Its attitude will be neither fearful nor vulgar. It will be, in short, a civilized voice in a civilized community.

CHAPTER TWO

The Present System

Over the past decade, a system of educational television has come into being that now includes stations covering nearly two-thirds of the population, a national program service, patches of interconnection, and above all a corps of devoted men and women. It is on that foundation that we propose to build.

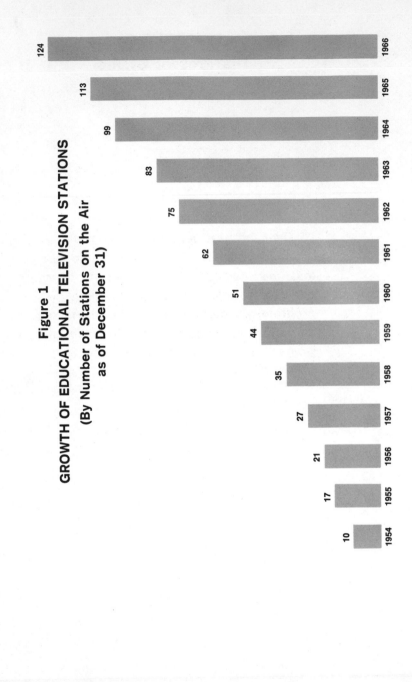

Figure 1

GROWTH OF EDUCATIONAL TELEVISION STATIONS

(By Number of Stations on the Air
as of December 31)

The Present System

Since the first educational television station went on the air in May 1953, the system has grown steadily and rapidly in size and in complexity. That growth over the years since 1954 may be seen in Figure 1. When the Commission began its deliberations little more than a year ago, there were 113 educational stations on the air; by the close of 1966 the number had risen to 124. A new frequency band in the 2500-megacycle range, intended to supplement the VHF and UHF stations for purposes of formal instruction, was opened in 1963. Since that time eighty-two applications have been filed with the Federal Communications Commission, and fourteen systems, utilizing eighteen channels, have gone on the air. More than a thousand closed-circuit installations are serving public and private education, industry, and government.

The great majority of the stations serving the general public are licensed to transmit over channels reserved for education by the Federal Communications Commission, although a few, such as WNDT in New York, operate on commercial channels under licenses which have been acquired for educational purposes by nonprofit corporations or other educational users. Like commercial television, although not to the same degree, the educational television system was initially lodged predominantly in the VHF band (Channels 2–13).* The proportion of VHF stations is declining (71 of the 124 stations) and the large majority of new stations are in the UHF band (Channels 14–83).

The 124 educational television stations on the air at the close of 1966 fall into four distinct categories:

School stations, licensed to school systems or school districts and brought into being primarily to serve elementary

*Channel 1, originally within the band, has since been assigned for other uses.

and secondary education. There are now 21 such stations.

State stations, licensed to state boards of education or similar state agencies. These, too, have been brought into being to serve primary and secondary education. They are frequently linked into state networks. There are now 27 such stations.

University stations, licensed to public rather than private colleges and universities. They have been brought into being primarily as an extension of ordinary university activities, including continuing education; in some cases they are also used as instruments for instruction in television or communications. There are now 35 such stations.

Community stations, licensed to nonprofit corporations.* These stations predominate in the large metropolitan areas, and in general are the largest and best-financed stations. There are now 41 such stations.

The distribution of these stations appears on page 105.

In their relationship to Public Television (as distinct from instructional television) the four categories as listed above are on an ascending scale. Almost without exception they broadcast Public Television programs. With respect to the local production of Public Television programs, the stations vary widely in the number of programs originated and the extent and diversity of program resources used in their production. The community stations as a group are most likely to look upon Public Television in the broadest range as their primary function, followed by university, state, and school stations in that order.

The coverage of the system must be measured separately for each of its two functions. The 124 stations are so located that their programs can theoretically reach an audience of approximately 125 million viewers, or two-thirds of the population. The full instructional system, which includes closed-circuit and 2500-megacycle stations, now reaches more than 10 million students, most of them in elementary schools. Total enrollment, which counts a student more than once if he attends more than one class taught with the aid of television, is estimated at 40 million.

*Except for WNYC–TV, New York, which is licensed to the city.

The instructional system aside, the quantitative account which has been given of the educational stations cannot be taken entirely at face value. The Commission has carried through, by means of financial questionnaires, a careful study of the system, and has benefited further from the visits conducted by the staff. The coverage figures must be modified to take account of outmoded transmitting equipment and the fact that many of the stations continue to operate below full authorized power.

Similarly, production equipment is both less than adequate in itself and less than adequately staffed in almost all stations. In general, the Commission estimates that over the system as a whole both capital investment and operating expenses are at approximately half the level required for the proper functioning of the system in the various roles that it now seeks to play: to accomplish properly what educational television now seeks to accomplish, and nothing more, would require that the funds available to the system be doubled. Even the better-supported stations, such as those in Boston and New York, are confronted with demands that far exceed their resources.

Program Sources

Programs intended for general viewing come to educational television from three principal sources and a variety of minor sources. The most important is National Educational Television (NET), with which almost all educational stations are affiliated. NET produces or procures from foreign sources (in particular the British Broadcasting Corporation) five hours of new programs a week, divided equally between cultural programs and public affairs programs. In addition, it has been providing two and a half hours each week of children's programs, and makes available its large library of programs for rerun.

New production is generally carried out by contract, since NET possesses no production facilities of its own. Roughly two-thirds is performed by staff or by independent producers, most of them in New York, and the remaining third by local educational stations, in all cases under close supervision by NET. Most payments for station production are awarded to stations in Boston, New York, San Francisco, Washington, D.C., Chicago, and Los Angeles, among others.

Another source of programs is represented by exchanges among local stations. Almost without exception, the programs are produced by the local stations themselves, and either by design or by chance are such as to be useful to other stations. Some of this program exchange is now carried out by the Educational Television Stations division of the National Association of Educational Broadcasters. One grouping of stations, the Eastern Educational Network (which will be considered in further detail below) also uses membership fees to obtain programs produced outside the system and circulates them among members.

Finally, the local stations produce programs for purely local use. These are usually produced at extremely low cost, using station equipment and station staff and with limitations of a few tens of dollars in out-of-pocket cost for each hour of programming. A few community stations — predominantly those already mentioned as contractors for NET — have mounted campaigns to raise funds both from industry and from their audiences, and are able to do something more in the way of local programming; it is those programs which are most likely to be exchanged with other stations.

For the average station, NET provides approximately half the general programming; film supplied free of charge by large industrial and commercial companies and local production provide about one-sixth each. These three sources account for approximately 80 percent of the total. The balance comes from a variety of sources: from program exchanges among the stations; from commercial networks and stations; from government agencies such as the Department of Defense, the Department of Health, Education, and Welfare, and the National Aeronautics and Space Administration; from the stations' own libraries; and so forth. This information is shown graphically in Figure 2.

Figure 2

SOURCES OF GENERAL PROGRAMMING
FOR AN AVERAGE ETV STATION, 1966

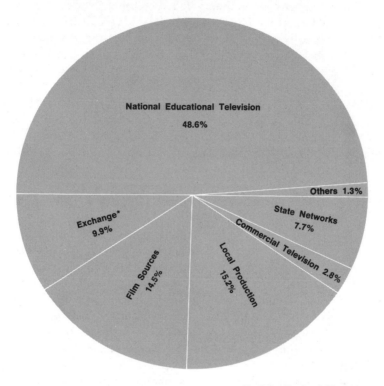

National Educational Television

48.6%

Others 1.3%

State Networks
7.7%

Exchange*
9.9%

Commercial Television 2.8%

Film Sources
14.5%

Local Production
15.2%

*Includes Regional Networks

TOTAL PROGRAM HOURS: 3,248

NUMBER OF STATIONS: 114

Source: One Week of Educational Television
April 17-23, 1966

Distribution

Electronic interconnection — the use of coaxial cable or microwave relay systems to link stations for simultaneous broadcasting, as is customary in commercial television — has not generally been used by educational television, primarily because of the large costs involved. NET distributes its programs by means of videotape, duplicating the tapes in its own facilities at Ann Arbor, Michigan, on a schedule that generally permits them to reach all stations within a two-week period for programs of timely interest.

The Eastern Educational Network distributes both by interconnection and by tape. Eight stations in New England and New York are linked electronically and form the heart of the system. Another thirteen stations in Pennsylvania, New York, and the District of Columbia are served regularly by tape. Other stations as remote from the East as KQED in San Francisco are associate members and benefit from program exchange on a less formal basis.

In addition, there are eight states which have statewide interconnections, and in most cases these are intended primarily for instructional televison, although they could of course carry Public Television as well. Some smaller interconnections exist, such as those which link San Francisco and Sacramento, California, and Oklahoma City and Tulsa, Oklahoma. Interconnections have been arranged from time to time on an *ad hoc* basis, notably along the Eastern seaboard. Most recently, the Ford Foundation has provided funds for the development of nationwide interconnected programs.

NET has been seeking for some time to create an interconnection system which would provide linkages east of the Mississippi. The motivation has been at least in part the steadily increasing cost of providing distribution by tape.

Since 1961, the Midwest Program for Airborne Television Instruction (MPATI) has used airplanes to transmit instructional programs within a radius of approximately two hundred miles of Montpelier, Indiana.

Sources of Operating Funds

Financial support for the educational television system is derived from many sources (Figure 3). By far the largest of these are state and local governments, acting through school systems, state boards of education or state instruments set up specifically for educational television, or state universities. For community stations, the funds are usually made available through contracts for the broadcast of programs to the schools. During the fiscal year 1965–66 state and local governments provided approximately $33.5 million for educational television. Most of those funds have been marked for instructional television, but they necessarily support programming for the home as well.

Direct support from the federal government has been made available by the Educational Television Facilities Act of 1962, which authorized a total of $32 million over a five-year period. In this the leadership and imagination of Senator Warren G. Magnuson, Chairman of the Committee on Commerce, and of other members of Congress have been major factors in fostering the growth and development of the educational television service. The funds are subject to certain limitations: they must be matched on an equal basis by a new station; they can be used only for certain facilities, such as towers, transmitters, and other transmission facilities; there is a limit of $1 million for any state. During the fiscal year 1965–66 funds to educational television stations from the Facilities Act amounted to approximately $7 million.

The Ford Foundation has been, since the inception of educational television, one of its prime supporters and for the community stations a life-giving source of funds.* NET is largely supported by the Ford Foundation, receiving $6 million annually of a budget that totals approximately $8 million. Since 1952 the Ford Foundation has also made available to the stations, on a matching basis, support which has so far totaled $30 million. These grants will terminate

*Overall, the Ford Foundation has given more than $120 million for the support of educational television.

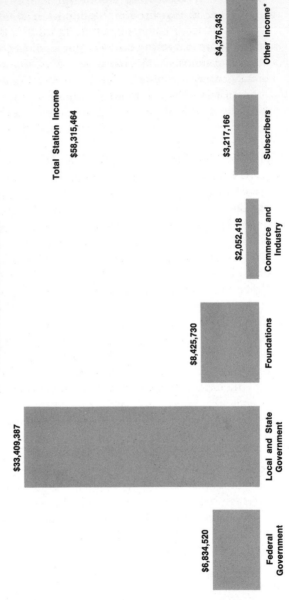

Figure 3
SOURCES OF STATION INCOME
Fiscal Year 1965-1966

Total Station Income
$58,315,464

$33,409,387

$8,425,730

$6,834,520

$4,376,343

$3,217,166

$2,052,418

Federal Government

Local and State Government

Foundations

Commerce and Industry

Subscribers

Other Income*

*Includes $1,095,131 in income from "Underwriting."

Source: Commission's Station Financial Questionnaire

shortly. The Ford Foundation granted nearly $8.5 million in this fashion during the fiscal year 1965-66.

Community stations customarily engage in sizable fund-raising activities, which bring in for some stations, such as KQED in San Francisco, a large part of their operating funds. During the fiscal year 1965-66 contributions to all stations from individuals amounted to approximately $3 million, and from corporations $2 million.

Finally, a variety of other sources contributed $4.4 million during the year. These included rental of facilities, consulting, and some program production not intended for broadcast by the stations. A portion also came through "underwriting," in which grants were made in support of specific programs by industrial or commercial organizations, which received on-air acknowledgment of their generosity. (When the Public Television system we propose has been created, it would seem desirable for the corporate support of educational television to take the form of general grants rather than the underwriting of specific programs involving on-air acknowledgments.)

Total income to the system, exclusive of NET, during the year was approximately $60 million.

The Need for Public Television

In brief, that is the system the Commission was asked to consider. Clearly there lie in educational television, as it now exists, elements of great strength. Undeniably it is a vital system, and a growing system as well. Undeniably, too, it has grave deficiencies, not all of which are financial. We have found, as we examined the stations, many which are weak and must be strengthened and many which have not yet dared adequately to elevate their sights.

We have interpreted our obligation as that of building upon the existing educational television system a new, vigorous, ambitious system of Public Television. What we have seen leaves us confident that the task can be accomplished.

CHAPTER THREE
The Proposal

The Carnegie Commission on Educational Television presents twelve recommendations, dealing primarily with Public Television but also treating elements of the total educational television system. Each recommendation is considered in this chapter.

The Stations

1 We recommend concerted efforts at the federal, state, and local levels to improve the facilities and to provide for the adequate support of the individual educational television stations and to increase their number.

Committed to diversity and to the differentiated audience, Public Television is deeply reliant upon the vigor of its local stations. Admittedly, like commercial television, it must have central sources of programming. But unlike commercial television, it will depend also upon a strong component of local and regional programming, and it must provide the opportunity and the means for local choice to be exercised upon the programs made available from central programming sources.

Yet we have seen that the local stations, as they are now constituted, are inadequate for the ends they must serve. There are not enough of them. Those that exist are inadequately staffed, inadequately equipped, and inadequately financed. Deficiencies affect the entire system; even the few stations that provide leadership for educational television wage a daily struggle for survival.

The Commission believes that the first task, upon which any further accomplishment must be built, is the strengthening of the local stations. We believe further that support for those stations must become available at all levels of government, augmented and stimulated by private initiative.

Support from just those sources has brought the present system into being. But mere existence is not enough. The stations that now constitute the system must be provided with the material and human resources that will enable them to operate efficiently and effectively, and their number must be increased until something close to national coverage is accomplished. They must be enabled to remain on the air over a full schedule, instead of going dark — as so many stations now must — during weekends, when they might be most viewed.

To be truly local, a station must arise out of a sense of need within a community, must have roots in the community, and must be under community control. It is not the physical location of studio and transmitter that is significant but the degree to which the station identifies itself with the people it seeks to serve.

In recommending further assistance for local stations from the federal government, we do not intend to suggest that the federal government assume responsibility for local stations. Rather, we recommend that federal assistance be made available as stimulus and support for local and state initiative. We recognize that local and state education budgets, from which funds for educational television are usually made available, are already strained near the breaking point, and that by themselves they cannot bear the full burden of station construction and station operation without losses elsewhere in the system. But that some funds should come from those budgets, so that the states and the localities may feel the pride and the responsibility of possession, we believe to be indispensable.

It is encouraging that there has been, in recent years, a marked elevation in state ambitions for educational television. Almost every state has some kind of plan for a state instructional system, and most plans include educational television stations of the sort being considered here. For those plans to come to fruition with local stations capable of more than straightforward classroom services, substantial federal support will be necessary.

The local support we contemplate, however, must go beyond the provision of funds. Public Television in particular is dependent for its well-being upon an identification with the community it serves. It must look for leadership to those who are leaders in the community. Those leaders must know its goals well enough to respect them and its mode of operation well enough to assist it.

We have found in our station surveys that many stations do not possess ties of this sort; that many boards of directors have lent nothing more than their names to the effort. We have found also that in those stations where directors and trustees take an active interest, the station itself is most likely to thrive.

In stations which are part of larger institutions such as school districts and universities we have found that the place of the station in the larger organization is too often at the bottom of the ladder. We consider this state of affairs to be particularly regrettable when the station is operated by a college or university. Within institutions of higher learning are to be found many of the talents and skills which are most needed by the television station, but they are infrequently brought to bear, for the station too often occupies no pride of place in the university hierarchy.

We recognize that it is somewhat deceptive to speak indiscriminately of "the local stations" as if they were all of a piece. As the system has come into being, there is a handful of relatively powerful stations which originate programs for their own audiences and for the audiences of educational stations in their own region or, at times, throughout the system. There are other stations which operate on modest budgets to meet modest ambitions.

We would like to see more strong stations, better distributed geographically, and we have planned with that objective. Our intention has been to create a means by which support — financial and substantive — may be made available to any community in which there exists substantial local desire and local means for a major station. We believe the process must be one of self-selection and that the power of decision should rest with the community itself and not with some agency outside the community.

The smaller stations, too, will require support commensurate with their needs. What is equally important, they will require a steady supply of Public Television programs to supplement their own modest production. It is to the means and the methods by which those programs will be produced that we next address ourselves.

The Corporation

2 We recommend that Congress act promptly to authorize and to establish a federally chartered, nonprofit, nongovernmental corporation, to be known as the "Corporation for Public Television." The Corporation should be empowered to receive and disburse governmental and private funds in order to extend and improve Public Television programming. The Commission considers the creation of the Corporation fundamental to its proposal and would be most reluctant to recommend other parts of its plan unless the corporate entity is brought into being.

The local stations must be the bedrock upon which Public Television is erected, and the instruments to which all its activities are referred. But there are needs that the local stations alone cannot meet. There must be effective leadership for the system as a whole. There must be means by which the stations communicate with each other, and with the public. There must be a means of performing services, as in the development of experimental programs and the recruitment of manpower, which are likely to be more efficiently carried out by an organization that can act for Public Television. There must be a system-wide process of exerting upward pressure on standards of taste and performance.

All of these are essential activities. Taken together, they can serve to weld Public Television into a seamless whole in all those aspects of its operation where it must be looked upon as a national institution, while yet leaving to the local stations their own individual autonomies in respect to their operations.

Because we contemplate federal assistance to Public Television on a far larger scale than at present, the pressing need arises to identify the manner in which federal funds will flow to the system. There is at once involved the relation between freedom of expression, intimately and necessarily a concern of Public Television, and federal support.

Recognizing areas of special sensitivity, the Commission is persuaded that a nongovernmental institution is necessary to receive and disburse at least a part of those funds. The purpose is not to escape scrutiny but to minimize the likelihood that such scrutiny will be directed toward the day-to-day operations of the sensitive program portions of the Public Television system. What we have sought to design is an institution that will represent Public Television, that in behalf of Public Television will receive and disburse federal, state, and, local government funds, as well as private funds, and yet will be free of political interference.

The institution itself, erected to serve the public interest, must be created and sustained in a manner that will permit it to assert the public interest. Toward the stations, too, its relation is a sensitive one, for it must support the stations, in some degree represent them, and yet be restrained from control or the appearance of control over them.

We propose that Congress act promptly to authorize and establish a federally chartered, nonprofit, nongovernmental corporation, to be known as the "Corporation for Public Television." The Corporation will be neither an agency nor an establishment of the United States government. It will be a free-standing institution, like other nonprofit corporations created to serve the public interest.

We propose that the Corporation be governed by a board of directors of twelve distinguished and public-spirited citizens, of whom six will be initially appointed by the President of the United States with the concurrence of the Senate, and the remaining six initially elected by those previously appointed. Thereafter, one-third of those appointed by the President and one-third of those elected will complete their terms at two-year intervals, with the President appointing two members every two years for six-year terms, and the entire board electing two members every two years for six-year terms.

In appointing and electing members, the President and

the board will be charged to choose those who will provide broad representation within the Corporation of the various regions of the country, the various professions and occupations, and the various areas of talent and experience appropriate to this enterprise.

The board of directors will appoint its own chairman and a full-time chief executive officer charged with the usual responsibilities of the chief officer of a nonprofit corporation. Since the Corporation will be a private corporation, all appointments to its staff will be made without regard to civil service requirements.

When organized the Corporation will be authorized at its discretion to do the following:

• To make contracts with national program-producing agencies and such local stations as have the necessary exceptional resources of talent and facilities for producing programs of more than local utility, and also to procure existing programs from domestic or foreign sources.

• To make contributions to local stations, as the Corporation deems desirable, to assist the stations in meeting the special expenses of producing and broadcasting programs of unusual significance and of primary interest and benefit to their local communities, beyond the assistance provided by other sources.

• To make contributions to selected stations so that they may procure capital facilities, beyond those provided for local stations with the assistance of the Department of Health, Education, and Welfare, or additional facilities required for Public Television programming.

• To make arrangements with companies operating suitable interconnection facilities (landlines or satellites) and provide the necessary financing for the distribution of these programs to all local stations which desire to receive and use them.

• To make contracts or grants with existing or new agencies (colleges, universities, television stations, nonprofit corporations, industrial laboratories, and the like) for conducting programs of training for technical, artistic, and specialized personnel required by the Public Television

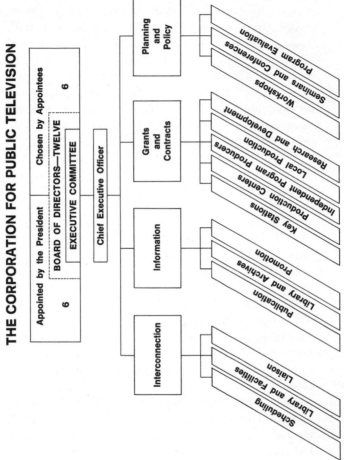

Figure 4
THE CORPORATION FOR PUBLIC TELEVISION

system and to assist research leading to the improvement of programming or of the technology of production and broadcasting.

• To promote the flow of information both within the system and outside it, to stimulate viewing of Public Television programs, to support a library of programs, and to cooperate in the establishment of archives in which materials of more than passing significance, from both Public Television and commercial television, will be held for those who have the desire or the need to make use of them.

• To perform such other functions as may be necessary, as changing technology or new organizational developments may require, to extend and improve the quality of the educational television service.

• To appoint and reimburse such expert consultants, advisory boards (including a board composed of representatives of educational television), or panels as are deemed necessary.

In general, the Corporation will act by means of grants to and contracts with stations within the system, entities of various kinds engaged in work associated with television, and colleges and universities. Except for its obligations in providing interconnection and dissemination of information, and perhaps for the establishment of archives, it should not act as an operating institution.

Figure 4 is a suggested table of organization for the Corporation.

The categorization given here omits, as any categorization must, any account of the general role the Corporation is expected to play. The Corporation should become, upon appointment of its board of directors and recruitment of its staff, the center of leadership for Public Television. By the very nature of its activities, it should be engaged steadily in establishing standards for Public Television. It should provide the means by which strong stations use their strength for the benefit of the entire system, and by which weak stations become strong.

For its support, it must inevitably look primarily toward the federal government, but by no means exclusively. The

Corporation should be prepared to solicit funds actively from private sources, such as industry and the major foundations. Its freedom from political control will be all the greater if it possesses resources for which it is not dependent upon the government, even though those resources constitute only a part of its total needs.

At the moment when it comes into being, the Corporation should be in possession of substantial financial resources for which it is not answerable to the government. It is our hope that from foundations and other private sources an endowment of no less than $25 million can be provided when the Corporation is chartered, for the free use of the Corporation as it takes shape and enters into operation, and as an assurance of stability for those who first join it and set it on its path.

Finally, the role of the Corporation must be expected to evolve over time. Public Television, like the entire communications industry of which it is a part, exists within the context of rapid change. It is part of a complex which includes far more than the transmission of sound and pictures. The technology upon which it is based is growing and altering, and it makes more visible each day the intimate relationships that link television as a vehicle of information and entertainment with libraries, archives, data processing and data transmission, the interplay of intellectual and artistic endeavors, social development, and social change. The historian of the future may look back upon these latter decades of the twentieth century as the years of a profound revolution in the art and the uses of communication. Television, and Public Television as one of its components, both affect and are affected by that revolution. The Corporation for Public Television must both help lead it and be moved by its imperatives.

What we propose here, in short, is an institution which must be vital and dynamic. We have said that we consider the creation of the Corporation fundamental to our proposal; we believe also that it can become an institution of great significance to American society.

Program Production

3 We recommend that the Corporation support at least two national production centers, and that it be free to contract with independent producers to prepare Public Television programs for educational television stations.

The principal responsibility of the Corporation will lie in supporting program production. The range of programming required by Public Television is wide. It must certainly include programs of high quality, dealing with themes for which there is an audience as wide as the system itself, and prepared with all the resources of television. The Commission recommends that the Corporation be enabled to contract for such programs and to pay for their production.

At present, programs intended for national use are produced almost exclusively by National Educational Television (NET) in New York. The Commission believes that NET, its staff and the experience that it has accumulated constitute an important resource for the Public Television system that is contemplated here. Certainly, one of the two national production centers which are proposed in this Report will be built upon NET. (Indeed, the continuation of NET activities is essential, for even after the Corporation is created the primary source of national programming will continue for some time to be NET.)

The Commission contemplates the national production centers recommended here as equipped ultimately to produce programs in their own studios and with their own staffs and facilities. The existence of stable and continuing producing organizations whose first loyalties are to Public Television appears to the Commission to be a necessary element in the system. Such centers, in addition to possessing capacities of their own, should subcontract some activities to encourage diversity of programming (for which, however, like NET, they will retain responsibility).

The mode of operation proposed by the Commission is one in which the national producing center will outline to the Corporation each year the general schedule it intends to meet and, in broad terms, the programs it proposes to produce. The Corporation will pass judgment on the proposal, and will provide support, including capital support where it is required, to enable the center to carry out those portions approved by the Corporation. The Corporation should encourage and support long-range planning as well, including two-year, three-year, and even five-year grants. It is clear that the degree to which any center is supported by the Corporation will depend on the persuasiveness of its proposals and on the degree to which its product meets standards established by the Corporation. But perhaps a third criterion is most important of all: since the programs will be offered to local stations for them to use or ignore as they see fit, the stations themselves will provide a continuing evaluation of programs each center supplies.

The Commission recommends at least two such centers, in part because it is reasonable to believe that at least two separate organizations should apply themselves to the production of national programming, and in part because the Commission believes that competition between two or more centers will act as a spur and will provide a basis for comparison. As contributory to the same process, the Corporation should be able to contract with other program producers, here and abroad, for single programs or for program series.

The national production centers will be, like the Corporation itself, nonprofit institutions. It is expected that they will derive the largest part of their income from the Corporation, but they will be encouraged to look to other sources of revenue, including grants from private foundations and commercial enterprises, and grants and contracts with departments and agencies of federal, state, and local government. Such grants might be used either to expand production or to extend budgets of programs produced under contract with the Corporation.

In general, the programming to be expected from the national producing centers will be comparable in subject matter to those now available from NET, although of greater diversity. Major theatrical and musical productions, documentaries on subjects of national concern or which require a national approach, programs dealing on a national scale with public affairs or with news commentary, are immediately appropriate. Light programs, children's programs, and programs of criticism and review, when they are planned on a scale that clearly requires exceptional talents and skills, are equally appropriate. The national programming, in short, is that which is likely to be of major interest to any station in the system, wherever it may be found.

The Commission has taken counsel with educational television stations, commercial stations, and independent producers, and commissioned a study of programming costs. It is our best estimate that the average cost for national programming of the kind and quality appropriate for Public Television will be approximately $45,000 an hour. This figure compares with current NET costs of approximately $20,000 an hour and commercial network costs of approximately $100,000 an hour.

Because Public Television is likely to have a reasonable number of low-cost programs, the $45,000 average leaves room for the occasional program that reaches or even surpasses slightly the commercial average. Commercial costs, too, include extremely high talent costs which Public Television need not consistently pay. Nonetheless, the $45,000 average does not allow for the truly high-cost program in excess of $250,000, such as the commercial production of *Death of a Salesman,* which the Public Television system might be extremely anxious to produce and which its audience would unquestionably welcome.

The Commission suggests that the possibility of truly high-cost programs for Public Television should not be foreclosed. The Corporation itself might be prepared to support an occasional such program. The production centers might turn to the private foundations, which may be receptive to proposals for the support of specified projects.

The ten hours of weekly programs upon which the estimates were based appears to us to be a reasonable figure. It is double the programming now provided by NET. It will enable each station to maintain a reasonable schedule of national programming, without being obliged (as the stations very nearly are now obliged) to use every program that is offered. The general question of the use of programs will be considered later in this chapter.

More-than-Local Production

4 We recommend that the Corporation support, by appropriate grants and contracts, the production of Public Television programs by local stations for more-than-local use.

Over the past few years several local stations, under vigorous leadership, have managed to build respectable production capacities and to finance a limited amount of ambitious Public Television programming. They have tapped every conceivable source of funds: the private foundations, the business community, and their audiences. They have produced programs under contract with NET. Under great difficulties, they have accomplished a great deal.

The programs thus produced are part of the lifeblood of today's educational television. WGBH in Boston is the flag station for a station grouping known as the Eastern Educational Network. Primarily because of WGBH's programming capacity, stations as far from Boston as KQED in San Francisco are associate members of the network. KQED itself makes programs available to other educational stations, as do WNDT in New York, WQED in Pittsburgh, KRMA in Denver, in recent months KCET in Los Angeles, and a few others.

There can be a special vitality in programs produced by such stations. They draw on the large reservoirs of persons of talent available in metropolitan centers, and they shape their programming for the known interests of their communities. In some cases the programs appeal to other stations in their immediate geographical region; in other cases the programs, such as Julia Child's widely acclaimed *French Chef*, find audiences throughout the country.

In estimating the cost and the amount of such programming, the Commission can provide no precedent to

serve as guideline. Programs of the sort now being produced are planned and created under conditions of such
extreme parsimony that they provide no basis for estimation. The need for such programming can only be measured
by the general statement that the system at present gobbles
up every one that is made.

The Commission has adopted a cost estimate of $30,000
for each hour of such programming, or two-thirds of the
costs of national programming, and estimates a need for
twenty hours of such programming a week.

Neither of these estimates need bind the Corporation.
In fact, no such sums can usefully be spent at present, and
it is highly questionable whether the stations or the talents
now exist which can produce twenty such hours a week.
These are, rather, goals which the Corporation might wish
to seek, and which it must be prepared to modify as experience accumulates.

The procedure for the production of such programs is
equivalent to that proposed above for national production
centers. Any station in the system would be able to make
proposals to the Corporation for single programs, sets of
programs, or program series. The Corporation would exercise its judgment on the proposals, and react accordingly.
As the process becomes established, stations with known
capacities would emerge, and would undoubtedly receive
the bulk of the contracts: the Commission hopes and
expects that in time twenty such stations, distributed
throughout the country, would be the prime producers
of programs for more-than-local use.

The process requires capital investments by the stations,
particularly those which lie outside the principal centers
of television production and cannot depend upon rental
arrangements. The Corporation must be prepared to advance funds for equipment and facilities, over and above
the stations' own equipment and facilities. Since the estimates of $30,000 an hour include charges for use of equip-
ment and facilities, the Corporation can expect to recover
its funds in the form of reduced charges for programs.

The equipment contemplated for these stations includes

modern, multi-camera, mobile color facilities, which will enable the producer to move at will outside the studio and use television at its most flexible and its most stimulating. Much of the somber and the static image which educational television has created for itself is the result of its inability to take its cameras beyond the four walls within which they have been fixed. Mobile units, able to proceed with dispatch to the place where the event is happening — to capture the event in its own environment — will create an undeniable vitality which must in time become identified with Public Television.

It will be stations so equipped which can be expected to provide the bulk of the real-time coverage that the system requires. The teach-in in Boston, the riot in Watts, the Senate or House hearing in Washington, all will be covered by the local station and made available to the entire system. The Corporation must be so organized as to respond quickly with assurances that any extraordinary costs will be met, and to put the resulting programs at once into the interconnection to be made available to all educational stations. The twenty stations — if that number is reached — which are ultimately built to this kind of capacity will provide special news coverage that will be unique to Public Television.

Local Production

5 We recommend that the Corporation on appropriate occasions help support local programming by local stations.

A third family of programs comprises those which are of interest entirely, or very nearly so, to the community served directly by a given station. Some categories are immediately obvious: news of purely local interest, civic affairs, local sports, local personalities. Others appear where the local station manager seeks them out: local musical or artistic talent, dramatic presentations prepared by little-theater groups, and a whole host of intellectual activities which may be found in colleges and universities.

It is clear that by producing and presenting such programs the station manager can provide an honest local flavor for his station and perform a comprehensive service for his community which is not now being performed by any other medium. Almost all stations, and particularly the community and university stations, make real efforts to produce programs of this sort. Except for a few stations which can absorb production costs in their other activities, the task is an almost impossible one. Local or not, programs require time for planning and some investment in costs of production.

The Commission recommends that the Corporation be prepared to support by grant a portion of this purely local programming. It should do so in response to specific proposals from the station which seeks such support; the criteria for approval should be in the first instance the judgment of the Corporation upon the station's ability to produce the programs and perhaps also the willingness of the station to match in some degree a Corporation grant with funds raised locally.

We have estimated that at an average a local station provided with $2000 weekly (or $100,000 annually) can produce one hour each week of such programming at a superior level of quality and content. A reliable income of that sort will enable the station to operate modest mobile equipment so that, like the larger and better-endowed stations, it may leave the confines of its studios and travel to events where they are taking place. It provides freedom to pay the costs of special talent and special material that may be needed for a given program.

The average of $100,000 a year is subject to wide fluctuations. Some stations simply do not possess the equipment or the skills or the opportunities to expend any such sum, and their requests to the Corporation will surely be more modest. Other stations, in great cities, will be able to justify requests for several hundreds of thousands of dollars, with which they can give extremely large audiences a kind of local service which is not now available to them. In each case, the Corporation must be prepared to exercise its best judgment.

We recommend that the Corporation be enabled ultimately to set aside $20 million annually for this purpose. At face value, this sum amounts to approximately $100,000 a year for each station we expect to be engaged in Public Television several years hence; in fact, it is a rough estimate of the funds that will be required to meet the varying justifiable needs of varying stations. As in previous estimates, the beginning figures are not likely to be at anything like this level, and the Corporation can plan to begin modestly and to alter its sights one way or another as experience accumulates.

The Full Program

The total effect of this recommendation and the two that precede it will be to provide for each station a body of programs from national production centers, key stations, and local production. In the first category there will be a steady supply of ten hours a week for each station. The second category adds approximately twenty hours a week.

The third category is somewhat more difficult to estimate. Strictly speaking, it adds an hour of local programming for each station. In reality, the system today exchanges some of this programming, and it is quite reasonable to expect that a Boston program built upon local cultural affairs, local talent, and even in some cases local civic events will have an audience elsewhere in New England and here and there in other areas. It does not seem unreasonable to suggest that one hour of such production per station adds up to five hours of availability — that is, that over the system as a whole each such program will be used in five stations.

The total is therefore thirty-five hours of programming each week. To this can be added whatever can be produced by the station's own staff and equipment, which at present provide most local programming. It is reasonable to expect that such staff-produced local programming will increase in both quality and quantity.

The figure of thirty-five hours might be measured against the total requirements for Public programming. These, of course, will depend for any given station upon its policy in general, and in particular upon the manner in which it divides its time between Public and instructional programs, and the hours it customarily remains on the air. In our own view, the Public Television schedule might well occupy most of the time between 5:00 P.M. and 11:00 P.M. on weekdays, between 9:00 A.M. and 11:00 P.M. on Saturdays, and between noon and 11:00 P.M. on Sundays. Allowing small portions of these periods for other services, the need can be estimated at fifty hours a week for a station seriously engaged in Public Television.

In practice, however, Public Television, unlike commercial television, may be expected to repeat programs in any given week. Freed from the necessity to attract maximum audiences at all times, Public Television would indeed be derelict if it attempted to pin its potential audience to the fixed schedule of commercial television. A first-rate play, made with extraordinary care at great expense, warrants at least three showings during the week — perhaps one or more on weekday evenings, another on Saturday night, and still another on Sunday afternoon. Something of the sort would appear to be a very real obligation for Public Television.

A station which chose to use six out of the ten hours of national programming in any week would thus have eighteen of its hours filled; ten of the twenty more-than-local programs might complete another twenty hours or more; five hours of local programs might complete another eight. The station is thus able to exercise wide choice and with its staff-produced programs and whatever it finds useful to accept from other sources fill without difficulty its fifty hours a week. Those other sources, in time, would almost certainly include the library amassed over the years by the Public Television system: great plays performed by great actors, or great music by great artists, do not lose their usefulness in a single week of presentation. By any standards, the system even at its beginning will be abundant; in time it would be fully commensurate with the needs of the system.

Interconnection

6 We recommend that the Corporation provide the educational television system as expeditiously as possible with facilities for live interconnection by conventional means, and that it be enabled to benefit from advances in technology as domestic communications satellites are brought into being. The Commission further recommends that Congress act to permit the granting of preferential rates for educational television for the use of interconnection facilities, or to permit their free use, to the extent that this may not be possible under existing law.

The word "interconnection" is usually taken to denote a system that links television broadcast stations to each other, and to central distribution points, by electronic means. There are at present three means of providing interconnection: by coaxial cable, which links stations by wire; by microwave relay, which links them by electromagnetic waves and a system of relay towers; and by satellite, in which electromagnetic waves are transmitted into space and relayed back to earth.* In practice, the continental interconnection is at present a combination of coaxial cable and microwave relay, to which satellite relay is added for transmission across the Atlantic and Pacific oceans. For the most part cable and microwave systems, which are collectively known as landlines, are leased from the American Telephone and Telegraph Company, and satellite services from communications carriers authorized to deal with the Communications Satellite Corporation (COMSAT).

Once in place, an interconnection can be used in two quite distinct ways. It can be used for *networking* — that

* Off-air transmissions, in which special antennas receive signals from a relatively nearby station for rebroadcast, also are sometimes used to interconnect stations.

is, to enable all interconnected stations in a given area (which may be the entire continent) to transmit at the same time a single signal emanating from a central point. Alternatively it can be used for *distribution,* in which case the interconnection becomes a rapid and efficient means of delivering a program from a central point to all potential users, any of whom can either play it immediately or record it for later use. In either case, the interconnection itself remains unchanged: the difference lies only in the manner in which the interconnection is being used.

The use with which the American public is most familiar is that of networking, for with minor exceptions the commercial system uses the interconnection almost exclusively in that manner. Where events of overriding national concern or interest are involved, the system is used for "live" networking — the event is transmitted over the interconnection as it takes place before the cameras. Live networking is also called upon for sports events, and for portions of national news programs; it is otherwise rarely used. By far the most common commercial use of networking consists of the transmission from some central point — almost exclusively New York or Los Angeles — of programs previously recorded on film or tape. This assures that affiliated stations within a given time zone will broadcast the same programs at the same time.

The need for live networking capability is as great for Public Television as for commercial television. It is likely that Public Television will seek instantaneous coverage of important events with more freedom than commercial television, for Public Television can make its decision entirely upon the significance of the event, where commercial television must weigh the event carefully against the disruption of its ordinary fixed schedules and consequent economic loss. Even for Public Television, the occasions when the system goes "live" may be rare. When they occur, however, they can become not only the best use of television but the most exciting and the most rewarding. Each station should have the opportunity of going "live" when the occasion warrants.

Ordinary networking of taped or filmed programs, inseparably linked with the concept of the single signal, appears to the Commission to be incompatible in general with the purposes of Public Television. It presupposes a single audience where Public Television seeks to serve differentiated audiences. It minimizes the role of the local station where Public Television, as we see it, is to be as decentralized as the nature of television permits. Public Television is justified in reconsidering the best uses of interconnection in terms of its own needs, rather than imitating thoughtlessly the familiar manner in which the commercial networks use it.

The Commission consequently proposes that Public Television look to interconnection primarily as a device for the distribution of programs. Whatever is produced within the system would be transmitted over the interconnection, according to a schedule made known in advance to station managers. There would be no expectation that the programs would be immediately rebroadcast by the local station (although of course there would be nothing to prevent such use). Instead, the local station manager would be expected to record those programs he might later use, ignoring the rest.

We wish to make it clear that what we recommend here is an attitude toward interconnection and not a rigid set of procedures. Beyond any doubt, Public Television must be fully prepared to use live networking when the occasion warrants. There is every reason for the system to use ordinary networking from time to time, when a production of outstanding merit or significance justifies an extraordinary effort to attract a large audience. The Corporation should be prepared to exercise judgment on these as on other matters. What we recommend is simply that the ordinary use of the system be for distribution rather than networking, and that the Corporation adopt attitudes toward interconnection consonant with that intention.

Interconnection and Satellites

The communications satellite promises to introduce a

new dimension into interconnection. A communications satellite is capable of receiving and retransmitting to earth a number of television programs simultaneously. Each television station would possess an antenna capable of receiving signals from the satellite, thus completing the link between the distribution point and the network of stations. Such a system would have greater capacity than the existing landline system. It would assist the commercial networks in solving time-zone problems, and it would perhaps provide for Public Television (as well as commercial television) a flexibility that would permit greater use of regional interconnected networks.

No such communications satellite yet exists that can transmit signals adequate for such service; communications satellites over the Atlantic and Pacific oceans deliver to the ground signals of such low power that extremely expensive antennas are necessary to receive them, putting them out of reach of local broadcasting stations. (As those satellites are now used, linkages between the ground antenna and the local stations are provided by conventional landlines.) There is little doubt, if any, that it is now quite feasible to put in orbit a communications satellite that will be capable of providing network interconnection. Policy questions remain to be resolved concerning ownership of such a satellite, the manner in which it will be operated, its integration with landlines, and its relationship to international agreements to which the United States is a party. The engineering required, however, is already at hand, and without doubt such satellites will be in operation within a very few years.

For the immediate future, we do not believe that the addition of the communications satellite affects our conclusions on the appropriate uses of interconnection. In the more distant future, when satellites may possess the capacity for direct broadcasting to the home, a new situation will arise; these possible uses of the satellite no longer constitute interconnection in the sense in which we have used the term.

At present educational television cannot afford complete interconnection. Interconnections linking all educational stations in the state have been established, usually for instructional television — although they can be and are also used for home viewing — in Georgia, Nebraska, and South Carolina, where they are leased from AT&T, and in Minnesota, Alabama, Maine, Oklahoma, and Oregon, where they are state-owned. Eastern Educational Television links eight stations in New England and New York on private facilities, and smaller linkages are found in several other states. In addition, *ad hoc* linkages have been made from time to time along the Eastern seaboard.

We have estimated the annual cost of a national leased interconnection, based on a complex of state interconnections, at $17 million. We have further calculated, on the basis of criteria drawn from the operation of existing state systems, that the portion of this cost that might reasonably be attributed to Public Television is approximately $9 million. We have used this latter figure as an estimate of costs to the Corporation, under existing circumstances, on the assumption that state and local funds, together with federal funds provided outside the Corporation, will cover state network costs.

It may well be, as we have already indicated, that these costs will be reduced by new technology, including satellite interconnection, and that in addition this new technology will provide a more copious service. It is difficult at this time to estimate the extent to which these costs might be reduced.

The Commission recommends that Congress take action which would make it possible to allow preferential rates for Public Television, whatever the communications facilities used, to the extent that this is not provided by existing law. The Federal Communications Commission already grants preferential telegraph and cable rates for the press.

So far as communications satellites are concerned, we recommend that Congress consider legislative directives that would make possible free satellite interconnection for educational television to the extent that this is not provided for under existing law. Proposals to this effect have recently been made, notably by the Ford Foundation, in response to a Notice of Inquiry by the Federal Communications Commission, which is considering policy and regulatory problems arising out of satellite developments.

We recognize the matter of common carrier rates to be intricate and of far-reaching consequence. Any changes must certainly undergo the scrutiny of the Federal Communications Commission, and possibly the scrutiny of Congress.

Flexible, copious, and low-cost interconnection, if a combination of satellite development (or other new technology) and preferential treatment can bring it about, might have major consequences for Public Television. Regional live interconnection would become entirely practical, and would extend the capacity of the system to use television where it is most effective. A channel might be held open at all times for national or international deliberative bodies such as the House and Senate, and the United Nations. Another channel might provide day-long and evening-long series of programs in adult education; still another could direct itself to preschool education. Such programs could be used at will by all stations, and would make immensely valuable the second educational stations now planned for major metropolitan areas.

Matters such as these, however, soon move beyond questions of interconnection to considerations of further technological developments.

Experimental Production

7 We recommend that the Corporation encourage and support research and development leading to the improvement of programming and program production.

In one respect at least Public Television possesses a great advantage over commercial television: it can enjoy the luxury of being venturesome. Unaffected by the large financial investments that are at stake in each commercial program, Public Television is free to experiment.

There are many ways in which this might be done. One is by providing a center — perhaps more than one — explicitly designed to create experimental programming, and free of other responsibilities. In the allied field of education there are prototypes in such institutions as Educational Services Incorporated, which engages in the production of experimental curricular material, and the Regional Educational Laboratories contemplated by the Office of Education, which will have somewhat similar obligations. In the field of motion-picture production, plans to create such a center have been announced by the National Council on the Arts. At these centers people of high talent are brought together with a view to experimentation; anything they produce can flow into the system for trial and evaluation. The procedure seems most appropriate for Public Television, and will be described in detail later.

Similar activities might be encouraged in universities, and particularly in those which possess educational stations. It is most fruitful to give some degree of freedom to those who are beginning to try their wings, as recent university accomplishments in experimental film-making have demonstrated. A Center for the Performing and Visual Arts, based on these concepts, is now planned for the State University of New York.

In national production centers and in key stations, little

more is required than an attitude of receptiveness toward experimentation, and the Corporation, through its support of those institutions, can do much to encourage that attitude. Here, in close contact with the exigencies of the schedule, experimentation takes place in the real atmosphere of broadcasting and of program production. The highly successful TV–Radio Workshop once sponsored by the Ford Foundation is an example of experimentation and development which made a real contribution to television.

Considering Public Television in its broadest sense, there is a clear need for experimental work designed to put television to use in communicating with citizens of our inner cities who have special requirements and special needs. Those requirements and needs are not being fully met today by the mass media, including television. Television as it now exists can provide no guidelines that will assist in establishing this communication. It is something that must be learned.

Wherever the experimentation takes place, and to whatever end it is directed, it must enjoy an environment hospitable to risk, to a search for new forms, and to creative work by persons of exceptional talent. It must look to the fullest exploitation and realization of television as a medium in its own right. It must think in terms of new audiences. In the end, it may be a means by which a whole world of creative talent, which now stands aloof from television, can begin to serve and to draw strength from the diverse audiences that Public Television will reach.

Technical Research

8 We recommend that the Corporation support technical experimentation designed to improve the present television technology.

The Commission is well aware that programs of research and development are in constant progress within commercial television and in industrial organizations which supply equipment for television. We anticipate that industrial enterprise will continue to carry the major burden of research and development bearing upon the improvement of television, and that its efforts will continue to yield steady advances.

We feel, however, that the Corporation for Public Television which we propose will have opportunities, and indeed responsibilities, to encourage or accelerate new television technology, particularly for the special purposes of noncommercial television. There may well be important opportunities ahead for encouraging developments that could have greater significance for noncommercial television than for commercial television. We also believe that a close relation between the Corporation and the world of technology is important so that it may keep abreast of the rapid changes that will continue to take place in television technology. If the Corporation is to deal adequately with the substance and form of programming of Public Television, with its economics, and with the new ways in which it might serve the public, it must be prepared to take advantage of the changing technological resources. We note also that opportunities exist for significant improvements in picture quality and reception for all television.

The Commission does not contemplate that the Corporation itself will conduct programs of research and development. What we seek for the Corporation is the capacity to sponsor or encourage research at a modest level. It is the possibility of a catalytic effect that leads us to favor such research rather than any belief that educational television should assume any major responsibility for advancing the technology of television. We propose that the Corporation be able to contract with research-and-development organizations, both public and private, for general investigations or for specific programs of applied research that might contribute to the advancement of both Public Television and instructional television.

From reports presented to it by its technical advisers, the Commission notes the following examples of technological changes or developments possible in the immediate future, or in the distant future, which could be important for educational television, if not for all television.

All educational television, for example, may be affected by developments in the storage and retrieval of television programs. The storage of television signals has been effected for the past ten years by means of magnetic tape. Both storage and playback are instantaneous, and the systems now in use can also freeze action. Costs are high: storage for color playback of broadcast quality requires an installation costing in excess of $75,000, and the tape itself (which can, however, be reused) sells at $225 for one hour of recording capacity. Below those prices, quality falls off sharply, and although videotape recorders are now available at approximately $1000, they are not professionally useful devices. Undoubtedly the price for quality videotape recorders will fall, through ordinary industrial advances, to something well below its present level, but it will remain some tens of thousands of dollars.

The technology of other kinds of storage devices, however, is advancing rapidly. One device under development bears to the videotape recorder the relationship of the long-play phonograph record to the audio tape recorder. The television signal is stored on tape or film at a central point, where a large investment in machinery has been made; the cartridges which are so produced could be sold at a few dollars each if adequate volume is achieved, and would be available for playback in the home, over the air, or through coaxial cable.

For some time the principal developments in low-cost storage have looked toward storage on magnetic tape. More recently, there has been a revival of work on motion-picture film, and there is great promise that 8-millimeter film, and perhaps even greater steps toward miniaturization, together with developments in the design of projection equipment, will make that older medium capable of storing information cheaply, efficiently, and with a minimum of bulk.

What is almost certain is that one kind of low-cost storage device or another will at some time become available to complete the armory of storage systems: the video-tape recorder will be used, at fairly substantial cost, for instantaneous recording and instantaneous or slightly delayed playback; the new devices will be economically available for delayed playback of preselected programs.

The significance of low-cost program storage of instructional television may be great, and will be considered in a later section of this Report. For Public Television, the development of low-cost storage joined with devices for home playback may alter the economics of program production by permitting part of the cost to be shared with those who wish to buy video records of the program for their private use. Even without home playback, low-cost storage may permit individual stations to amass sizable libraries of television programs for reuse at will.

Systems in which television programs are delivered to the user by coaxial cable rather than by broadcast are also of great potential significance. Existing cables can carry twelve channels into the home, and the capacity can be easily extended to twenty channels or more. Since major capital investments are necessary, wired systems in the form of Community Antenna Television (CATV) came into being initially only in those areas where topographical barriers or distance from the transmitter precluded ordinary broadcast service. In such areas, entrepreneurs seized the opportunity to erect large and sensitive antennas to receive the programs, and at a modest charge to the public redistributed the programs by cable. More recently, the desire for a wider choice of programs, network and non-network, and the sensitivity to interference of broadcast color signals have made similar services attractive in many more locations, and CATV is beginning to penetrate densely populated areas.

There is presently public debate as to whether these systems should be permitted only to retransmit programs initially transmitted by open-circuit stations (with some minor exceptions). Wired systems — CATV or closed-circuit — are conceivable in which programs would be originated for initial use on the wired system itself. Since with cables the problems of frequency allocations do not arise, the technological limitations on the number of programs any set can receive are those of the set itself. By law all sets must now be built with a capacity for eighty-two channels, and hence nothing prevents the delivery of eighty-two channels to the home but the economics of wiring the home and creating the programs — which may, indeed, be a formidable or even a forbidding barrier.

The Commission has not studied the effect on local television stations of programs relayed by CATV systems from other stations outside the coverage areas of the local television stations; nor has it studied the public policy questions involved in the origination of TV programs by wired systems, whether such systems are CATV or closed circuit, and the distribution by these systems of programs to the public for a fee.

Reference was made earlier to the possibility — in perhaps a decade or less — that satellite engineering may permit direct broadcasting to the home. If and when that time arrives, the local station could be bypassed. In that event there will arise a fundamental question in public policy, because at that time the issue would be "localism" — i.e., the preservation of free local broadcast services — versus a tightly centralized control of all broadcast news and programming. That issue would have to be resolved by the American people. The Commission itself was forced to consider the possibility that we were laboring to design a system which might someday become obsolete. In the end, the Commission assumed that the concept of Public Television with its stress upon the principle of "localism" would be sustained, and hence this concern was unwarranted.

Since television is so likely to be affected by technological advances, it is essential that the Corporation be enabled to participate, in however modest a degree, in the process of change itself. Only by participating will Public Television possess some confidence that it can be at least in part the master rather than the servant of change.

Recruitment and Training

9 We recommend that the Corporation undertake to provide means by which technical, artistic, and specialized personnel may be recruited and trained.

An important part of the whole task for Public Television is the provision of opportunities for talented persons in all branches of programming and of technology to develop their crafts through association with production centers and broadcast stations. We believe that these centers should systematically provide in-service training and the Corporation should help them do so.

Public Television should actively recruit and develop a full range of personnel including producers, writers, directors, graphic artists, scenic designers, music specialists, technicians, and production and business managers. The Corporation for Public Television should sponsor fellowship programs designed to attract promising talent into in-service training programs conducted at production centers and into the experimental centers described earlier. In addition, the Corporation should provide stipends for senior fellows — men and women of experience and distinction — to spend periods in residence at the centers we have described. In commercial television, the Columbia Broadcasting System has provided similar stipends for academic study.

It is proposed that professionals from the several worlds of performance and expression, including television, the theater, and journalism, be invited to the centers for varying periods of time to acquaint themselves with new techniques, to regenerate their powers, and to contribute their own inventiveness to the general welfare of Public Television. Universities could help by establishing fellowship programs for television similar to the Nieman Fellowships in Journalism at Harvard.

We suggest that individual educational television stations consider appointing advisers from the community to review their programming, serving as individual consultants or as members of advisory panels. We believe that such an arrangement can provide, in terms of Public Television, a more discriminating and useful standard of judgment than that of the conventional ratings so widely used in commercial television today.

We believe also that there will be a need for an independent journal devoted to Public Television which will deal creatively and critically with all aspects of the system.

To the Corporation functions listed in this section there should be added such others as the dissemination of information, the preservation of archives, and the promotion of programs.

The Commission has not attempted to make careful estimates of the costs of such activities, or of the general costs of the Corporation itself. In the Commission's view, each must be looked upon as an evolving activity, in which the Corporation will take careful initiatory steps and be prepared to exercise judgment on further developments.

Only so that the accounting may be complete, we have set down a figure of $15 million a year for all the activities considered here and in the two sections immediately preceding. The Commission does not imply that initial costs will be in anything like that amount. We expect rather that at the outset they will be far closer to $5 million for each of the first few years. Even this reduced figure is an approximation, and should be viewed in that light.

Revenues

10 We recommend that Congress provide the federal funds required by the Corporation through a manufacturer's excise tax on television sets (beginning at 2 percent and rising to a ceiling of 5 percent). The revenues should be made available to the Corporation through a trust fund.

In the sections immediately preceding, we have stated the principal activities of the Corporation and have estimated in broad terms the costs of each. In round figures, these come to $80 million a year for programming and capital amortization, $9 million for interconnection, and $15 million for other activities, including operating expenses of the Corporation itself. The grand total is thus $104 million a year. These are our best estimates of the operating level of the Corporation when it reaches equilibrium, perhaps as much as ten years from the time of its establishment. They must be qualified also by recognition that the Corporation will be an evolving institution during that period — an institution which will shape itself as it grows.

We have estimated also the costs to the Corporation during the first few years of its existence. During that period, the Corporation will have sizable capital costs, incurred in the development of its own facilities, those of the national production centers, and of certain key stations. Most of these costs may be considered to be in the nature of a revolving fund, since they will be recovered in the form of reduced charges to the Corporation for programs and later reexpended to replace facilities as they wear out or become outmoded.

Our estimates for each of the first four years of the Corporation's operation show capital costs of $11 million, programming costs of $31 million, interconnection costs of $7 million, and administrative and other costs of $7 million; the total for each year being $56 million. These are the costs for which the Corporation must look to the federal government.

We are thus led to the conclusion that the Corporation will require from federal funds approximately $40 million in its first year and $60 million a year for the following years, allowing for a moderately rapid buildup.

For these funds, within the area in which Public programming is most sensitive to government involvement, the Commission cannot favor the ordinary budgeting and appropriations procedure followed by the government in providing support from general funds. We believe those procedures are not consonant with the degree of independence essential to Public Television. We have relied, therefore, upon a mechanism which Congress has used repeatedly in the past, by which revenues from clearly specified sources are collected by the government and the proceeds (or amounts equal to the proceeds) are paid into or credited to an account or trust fund and held in the Treasury for use in carrying out specified purposes as provided in the statute. Such mechanisms maintain intact the ultimate Congressional control over the use of public funds but permit the funds to be disbursed outside the usual budgeting and appropriations procedures.

We wish to repeat our reasons for invoking this mechanism. The combination of a private, nongovernmental corporate structure and a federally financed trust fund permits the Corporation to be free of governmental procedural and administrative regulations that are incompatible with its purposes, and to avoid the overseeing of its day-to-day operations that would be a natural consequence of annual budgeting and appropriations procedures. The Corporation and the trust fund are jointly essential to the insulation of Public Television from the dangers of political control. At the same time, Congress retains the power to terminate the arrangement at any time; its ultimate control over the expenditure of public funds is not impaired.

For the source of funds for the Corporation, the Commission recommends a manufacturer's excise tax on television sets as the most appropriate and least onerous. It is not a new tax; from 1950 to 1965 there was a 10 percent excise tax on sets. It is easily specified and easily administered. The tax would, of course, be passed along to the purchaser in the form of a small increase in the price of any new set he might buy; over the years of useful life of the set the annual additional cost will be extremely small. If it is at all a regressive tax, it is only mildly so; high-income families tend to buy more television sets and replace them more often. Finally, the improved service made possible by the tax directly increases the real value of the set.

The current value of television sets manufactured annually indicates that a tax rate of 2 percent will meet the requirement for $40 million during the Corporation's first year of operation, and a tax rate of 3 percent will meet the requirement of $60 million a year for each of the succeeding three years. We would expect that legislation will specify those initial rates and that as needs increase thereafter, the Corporation will seek increases in the rate up to the ceiling (and equilibrium) rate of 5 percent.

For the least costly black-and-white sets in general use, which have lifetimes of approximately seven years, the initial excise rate of 2 percent works out to approximately 30 cents a year to the purchaser over the lifetime of his set. The maximum rate of 5 percent comes to 75 cents a year over that lifetime, or 1½ cents a week.

Color sets, at present prices (which will presumably be reduced in the years directly ahead) will incur an additional charge to the user over the useful life of the set of approximately $1.00 a year at the initial rate, and $2.50 at the maximum rate — less than 5 cents a week at most.

In our view, these figures constitute a forceful justification for selection of the excise tax as the most appropriate method of financing Public Television. The financial demand upon the viewer is small, and administration of the tax is without complication.

The Ford Foundation, to which educational television

owes a historic debt, has proposed a satellite system (and an independent corporation to manage it) which would provide free interconnection for educational television and would also provide, out of profits from commercial activities, financial support for educational television. We see no conflict between such proposals and the organization and plan we present. We heartily approve in principle the objective of reducing the cost of interconnection for educational television, as we have already stated. We cannot be certain that the ingenious Ford proposal or similar plans would yield benefits large enough to provide more than a small part of the funds needed by educational television, but we do suggest that any funds that might become so available be applied to reduce the ceiling on the excise tax we recommend. We also conclude that the Ford Foundation proposal for a domestic satellite corporation, as well as other proposals recently presented to the Federal Communications Commission, involve issues of public communications policy that go beyond the scope of this Commission, and indeed beyond the domain of educational television. We feel that the Carnegie Commission should not undertake to formulate conclusions on these contending issues, and we urge that the adoption of a program to strengthen educational television not be delayed for their resolution.

Other proposals for financing Public Television have been laid before the Commission and considered at length. Among them were proposals for the imposition of license fees for the use of television sets (perhaps the most common procedure outside the United States for the financing of television); for removing restrictions which prevent educational television from accepting advertising; for conversion of educational television to some kind of pay television, or alternatively for the assignment of rights to operate pay television systems as a means of financing educational television; for gross revenue or franchise taxes upon commercial television; and for a procedure by which ordinary income taxes paid by commercial television would be earmarked for the support of educational television. None of these appeared to be as appropriate, as manageable, and as equitable as the excise tax.*

The Commission expects that the Corporation will receive funds from private sources and from foundations. In our rough accounting, we set the figure at $4 million annually. We expect such funds to serve several purposes. We have already expressed the hope that the major foundations will also be responsive to appeals from the Corporation for funds with which to produce special high-cost programs beyond the Corporation's normal budget. We have strongly recommended that the Corporation actively seek to accumulate an endowment, the income from which will give it areas of independence from government funds.

Concurring opinion of Mr. McConnell of the Commission:

I am not sure that I agree with the opinion of the Commission that there is a need for so extensive a Public Television service. Nevertheless, I am impressed by the sincerity and ability of my associates, and I, therefore, concur in the general conclusion on this point.

I am sorry, though, that I cannot completely concur in the recommendation for the imposition of an excise tax. As proposed, that tax would apply to the sale of television receivers, but not to the use of the airways by the holders of television licenses. I quite agree that if Public Television is to be financed in major part by the federal government, it would be highly desirable to avoid year-to-year appropriations by the Congress. The political implications of these are apparent. And certainly there should be complete divorcement of the programming and other functions of the Public Corporation from the government.

In effect, our proposal for an excise tax on television sets would tax the mass of the public, whose program preferences determine the television we have, to provide another service we believe they should have as well.

I suggest that those who are licensed to use the airways in the "public interest" — the television stations — should at least share in the cost of Public Television. If they should pay a franchise tax for that purpose, we can assume, as in the case of the tax on television sets, that this would be passed along to the purchaser — the advertiser. Perhaps it is the advertiser, with his basic test of program content, to whom we refer (page 13) when we speak of "acceptability — which . . . keeps commercial television from climbing the staircase." If this is what has brought about the need for Public Television, it would seem to me to be equitable that the advertiser bear a part of the cost, so that television could realize the promise for it so ably and so eloquently set forth in the Commission's Report.

We are hopeful that foundations will provide the Corporation with at least $25 million.

We expect that the Corporation will invoke matching provisions in making grants to local stations whenever it finds such provisions to be appropriate. It is our belief that a local station which has major ambitions in programming should certainly be encouraged and assisted by the Corporation but that it should also be obliged in some degree to exert itself in meeting part of the additional cost.

The total revenues to Public Television programming may therefore be expected to be somewhat greater than those provided by government funds. The Corporation itself will have the use of private money, and the stations may be expected to add resources they themselves have been able to procure. Federal funds, however, must be the mainstay of the system, and the Corporation will not be viable without federal support of approximately the size recommended here.

The Total System

11   We recommend new legislation to enable the Department of Health, Education, and Welfare to provide adequate facilities for stations now in existence, to assist in increasing the number of stations to achieve nationwide coverage, to help support the basic operations of all stations, and to enlarge the support of instructional television programming.

The Corporation for Public Television, as we have presented it here, is designed explicitly to act in those parts of educational television which are sensitive to the danger of political involvement and control. The activities of the Corporation, it is clear, depend upon a strong substructure which the Corporation itself is not intended to provide. The Corporation does not seek to assist in providing the basic facilities or the operating costs required for basic operation, much of which is instructional, nor does the Corporation propose to support the creation of new stations.

Those needs should not be ignored. As we have noted earlier, the existing stations are neither adequately equipped nor adequately staffed. They cover theoretically only two-thirds of the nation, and in practice even less. Many of them lack funds to remain on the air during periods when Public Television would be of greatest service. Although they act primarily in instructional television, their resources do not permit them even to provide an adequate instructional service.

The Commission believes that instructional television, like Public Television, requires far greater financial support than it now enjoys, but we have not attempted to engage in a detailed study of instructional television, and we cannot reasonably provide guidelines nor estimate costs. We believe, however, that the substructure of Public Television is roughly equivalent to the substructure instructional television would need, if it were to be supported as fully as it should be. We have estimated the cost of that substructure, common to the two parts of the educational television system.

We will present here a model of an educational television system which will provide coverage for approximately 95 percent of the population, omitting only those areas where population density is so low that any television service becomes uneconomic. We have assumed that each state will wish at least one station capable of preparing instructional programs of high quality, and that each large metropolitan area will require a substantial programming capability for instructional television. The Commission wishes to emphasize that what we will consider is only one of many possible models. We believe we have arrived at a system which is both workable and highly serviceable, but not necessarily uniquely so.

The full system, as we estimate it, will include a total of 380 stations.* Of this number, 43 will be second stations in 43 major metropolitan areas. Of the total, we propose 60 flag stations to provide each state with at least one station capable of major production in instructional programming and a few large states with two. We expect approximately 75 smaller stations, capable of some substantial instructional programming. In addition, there would be 75 stations of modest programming capability and a further 127 stations which would be little more than transmitters and towers.

Over a period of years the capital and operating funds flowing into the system would make it possible to achieve the full model we suggest. The succession of annual capital grants will finance the full system of 380 modernized and well-equipped stations. The annual cost of maintaining this ultimate national system, including amortization and operating costs, is $166 million exclusive of the $104 million attributed to the Corporation.

*Apart from the number of stations projected under this particular model, localities over this number may wish to have, or indeed may need, educational television stations. The costs of such stations are not included in these estimates.

It is highly unlikely that costs of this size can be met by state and local governments, which provide most of the cost of the existing educational television substructure. If such a system is to be brought into being, it will require substantial federal support. The Commission recommends that such support be forthcoming, by means of the ordinary procedures of the government acting through the Department of Health, Education, and Welfare.

The figures can conveniently be summarized in two tables. The first of these shows annual expenditures, including capital costs, over the first four years of the system, postulated on a buildup of the system which we consider to be rapid, but not excessively so:

Costs and Sources of Funds for System

(First four years, annual average)

	Total	Corpora-tion	HEW	Other
	(millions of dollars annually)			
Capital Costs	66*	11	37	18
Station Operations:				
Direct Public Programming Costs	19	19†	—	—
Other Costs	64	—	30	34
Production Centers	12	12	—	—
Interconnection	10	7	1	2
Public Television Corporation (non-broadcast activities)	7	7	—	—
TOTAL	178	56	68	54

NUMBER OF STATIONS AT BEGINNING OF PERIOD = 150‡
NUMBER OF STATONS AT CLOSE OF THREE YEARS = 240

* Includes $2 million per year for production centers.
† Including only operating component of cost of national programs at key stations.
‡ Projected to January 1, 1969.

As this table shows, during the first four years the annual average cost is estimated at $178 million, of which $56 million would come from the Corporation, $68 million from the Department of Health, Education, and Welfare, and $54 million from state and local government and private sources.

The second table shows annual expenditures at equilibrium, which we have assumed to occur in 1980. In this table, it is assumed the system is completely built and no capital costs, aside from amortization of existing equipment, are included:

Costs and Sources of Funds for System
(1980)

	Total	Corpora-tion	HEW	Other
	(millions of dollars annually)			
Amortization	57	6	34	17
Station Operations:				
Direct Public Programming Costs	51	51*	—	—
Other Costs	107	—	53	54
Production Centers	23	23	—	—
Interconnection	17	9	4	4
Public Television Corporation (non-broadcast activities)	15	15	—	—
TOTAL	270	104	91	75

NUMBER OF STATIONS IN 10 YEARS = 380

* Includes $29 million operating component of $31 million for national programs from key stations.

After the system has been developed over a period of years to an equilibrium stage, its annual costs will amount to $270 million, of which $104 million will come from the Corporation, $91 million from the Department of Health, Education, and Welfare, and $75 million from other non-federal sources.

These tables include assumptions in regard to matching provisions that the Department of Health, Education, and Welfare might wish to apply. Those assumptions were necessary to the preparation of the table, but are not intended to be more than suggestive of the course of action the Department might consider. Funds listed as "Other" are expected to come primarily from local and state governments, augmented by private and foundation contributions. Not included are funds that might be made available to the Corporation by such government agencies as the National Foundation for the Arts and the Humanities or by other sources.

Since some time must elapse before the full system begins to come into being we propose that in the interim Congress act to extend and amend the present Educational Television Facilities Act of 1962, which will otherwise expire with the present fiscal year. In particular, we urge that in extending the act Congress liberalize the requirements which limit funds flowing to any single state, and that it make funds applicable to the purchase of the full range of facilities and equipment, rather than limiting them, as it does now, primarily to towers, transmission equipment, cameras, and video recording equipment. Such extension will permit the system to grow steadily, as it has been growing in recent years, although not as rapidly as we submit that it should grow.

In making these proposals, the Commission calls attention to its belief that in this area, as in Public Television, the participation of the state government and of the local community is an essential factor. The level of state and local support that we propose, to be matched against federal assistance, is somewhat greater than what is now provided, but not excessively so; the Commission believes that a state which wishes to operate more stations than it now does should be prepared to contribute to their support to a somewhat greater degree.

The Commission wishes it understood that its twelve recommendations are not contingent upon the specific financial model it has just described. The model has been designed merely as an aid in estimating costs. The recommendations are based on the more general conviction that the public interest calls for a viable, adequately supported educational television system, and that federal participation in assuring its creation is both appropriate and desirable.

The educational television system so created would serve as a foundation for both Public Television and an expanded instructional service. Operating costs provided by the federal, state, and local governments, with the assistance of private individuals to community stations, would enable the stations to provide a basic instructional system and some local elements of the Public Television system. A flag station would in addition be enabled to provide more ambitious instructional programs for its own use and for the use of other stations in its state and region.

We believe that from this basic system would also come the bulk of the programs which are neither distinctly Public nor instructional in nature. Certain programs for adult education fall within this broad category, as do special service programs such as those addressed to doctors and nurses, those intended to stimulate such activities as Civil Defense or to communicate between the general public and various agencies of federal, state, and local government, and programs in household economics or market advice directed toward housewives. University stations might be expected to play special roles in providing programming of this general sort.

The Commission emphasizes the close relationship between the Public Television system it has proposed and the recommendations embodied in this chapter. It would be difficult to create a Public Television system such as that proposed in this Report, with its great reliance on local stations, unless the stations themselves can escape the pressures of penury and can equip themselves sufficiently to contribute to Public programming and to transmit an acceptable signal. It would be discouraging to create such a system in the knowledge that many of those eager to respond to it are not within range of an educational television station. The Commission does not believe that its system of Public Television is wholly dependent upon actions of the kind recommended in this chapter, but without those actions the system would certainly be less than it might be or should be.

Instructional Television

12 We recommend that federal, state, local, and private educational agencies sponsor extensive and innovative studies intended to develop better insights into the use of television in formal and informal education.

This Report and almost all its recommendations refer primarily to Public Television, and only upon occasion take note of instructional television. Yet to have attempted to maintain a rigorous separation between the two would have been at once unrealistic and futile. The two services share the same substructure, are part of the same educational television system, and at times are so inextricably intermingled that to speak of one is at once to force the other upon our attention. Thus, whether it chose or not, the Commission found itself repeatedly dealing with instructional television.

The general attitude of the Commission toward instructional television was recognized to be ambivalent. That there resided within television the power to make massive contributions to formal education was clear. That from time to time, and from place to place, instructional television has made impressive contributions, was readily conceded. Some of them are of considerable significance and breadth: the Chicago Junior College of the Air, the Hagerstown experiment, the extensive and ambitious South Carolina instructional system, and the Midwest Program for Airborne Television Instruction come at once to mind. But the Commission, and most of those who either appeared before it or were interviewed in the field, clearly believed that the role played in formal education by instructional television has been on the whole a small one, and that nothing which approached the true potential of instructional television has been realized in practice. Late in its deliberations, the Commission found its views reinforced by *Learning by Television*, published under the sponsorship of the Fund for the Advancement of Education, in which conclusions were reached that were certainly no more favorable than the Commission's own.

Since the views adopted by the Commission in relation to Public Television are clearly such that they maximize the role of the local station and lead to steps that will strengthen the local station, implementation of the recommendations of the Commission would tend toward general improvement of instructional television as well. A station which enjoys adequate financing, possesses modern facilities, and has attracted talented leadership and staff will inevitably be in a position to provide better programming for instructional television. Strengthening the components of the system strengthens both services the system provides, whether it is designed to do so or not.

The Commission believes, however, that the deficiencies in instructional television go far beyond matters of staff and equipment. It is of much greater consequence that instructional television has never been truly integrated into the educational process. Instructional television, like instructional radio and instructional motion pictures before it, lies outside the process, put to incidental or occasional use as ancillary material. With minor exceptions, the total disappearance of instructional television would leave the educational system fundamentally unchanged.

Even the claims made for instructional television by its most passionate defenders are in their essence defeatist. It is maintained that students learn as well from television as by conventional means, or that television can educate more cheaply. Such statements scarcely intimate that there is a powerful new medium of communication capable of making its own impress upon the process of education.

One accomplishment of instructional television, desirable if it stimulates appropriate action, has been to make evident shortcomings in the training and the support of teachers, clearly permeating the entire public educational system. Teachers who appear on television are usually men and women devoted to their calling, and responsive to their pupils; yet they must frequently struggle with a badly prepared syllabus and textbook, and without the variety of teaching aids, new and old, which a vigorous educational system might easily provide for them. It is not so much the deficiencies of instructional television that are laid bare, but the deficiencies of public education itself.

In short, the Commission believes that instructional television must be regarded as an element in the total educational process. The question must be asked whether, in a given educational context, television has a role of its own to play in relation both to a set of educational objectives and to the full battery of educational tools available. If television contributes to the quality of education, or makes possible a greater quantity of education, it will take its place as a tool of education, but it is in those terms that it should be approached and ultimately judged.

In its consideration of technological advances, the Commission has dealt at times with matters of considerable significance to instructional television. The most important of these are the low-cost storage devices, whether by television or by motion-picture techniques. The outstanding characteristic of such devices is that they promise to return to the classroom the flexibility that the present use of open-circuit broadcasting denies it. The teacher can select the program, play it at the moment of his own choosing, replay it at will in whole or in part, interrupt it for his own comments — in sum, fit the program to the needs of his own classroom as he understands them.

Should such devices come into general use, they will alter the manner in which the local educational television station serves the schools, as they might alter the use of closed-circuit television or point-to-point broadcasting over the 2500-megacycle band, and perhaps ultimately inhibit speculations which look toward broadcasting from satellites direct to antennas on school-building roofs.

But it is unlikely that the total need for instructional television emanating from outside the classroom will diminish. The development of instructional television within

the full context of education will make the schoolroom need
for television even greater than it is now. Much of that
need — indeed, that very part of it now satisfied by open-
circuit television — will be provided by other television techniques. Open-circuit television itself will then be freed to
provide material which cannot be brought to the school
in any other way: the material that must be handled and
moved quickly if it is to have real value, such as that for
use in current affairs courses. Properly used, television can
bring a liveliness and an immediacy to education that no
other medium can provide.

More fundamentally, the manner in which an instructional program is distributed is secondary, so far as its
service to education is concerned, to the manner in which
it is produced. It is the primary intent of the Commission
to strengthen the program-producing capabilities of educational television, at the level of the local station, the major
station, and the national production center. The purpose
is to improve Public Television, but inevitably the new
capabilities will spread into instructional television, for
the two parts of the system will never be discrete. The
local station with its strengthened production capability
will serve local school needs more effectively than ever
before.

From all these considerations, the Commission has made
two recommendations which directly concern instructional
television. One of them, discussed in the preceding section,
deals with the substructure that serves Public and instructional television alike. In addition, we recommend here a
major program of research and development in instructional television, designed to discover, within the full context of education, the manner in which television can best
serve education.

Such a program is clearly within the area of responsi-
bility of the Department of Health, Education, and Welfare.
The Office of Education now supports some research which
would contribute toward a full program. The Regional
Educational Laboratories now being established under the
Elementary and Secondary Education Act of 1965 might

well undertake a major share of the broader research which is required. Parts might also be carried out by local stations, supported by state and local funds; indeed, an ambitious program conducted in close association with existing educational establishments is a most promising procedure. It is, moreover, highly desirable that commercial enterprises, and in particular those now being created by the combination of educational and industrial organizations, should play a major role.

Above all, the Commission wishes to make it clear that the relatively small portion of this Report devoted to instructional television must not be taken as a measure of the Commission's estimate of its value. On the contrary, the Commission believes strongly that a television service which does not include a strong instructional component, along with commercial television and Public Television, is totally inadequate to the American need and purpose.

CHAPTER FOUR
The Promise

The system of Public Television proposed by the Commission is regarded as a whole, and its consequences and goals, as they relate particularly to programming for Public Television, are considered at length.

The Promise

In the preceding chapters there has been erected, piece by piece, a Public Television system of a new and different kind. It is not the educational television that we now know. It is not patterned after the commercial system or the British system or the Japanese system or any other existing system. We have attempted to design something that corresponds to American traditions and American goals, that can coexist amicably with commercial television, and that together with commercial television can meet the highest needs of our society.

The New Shape of Educational Television

These, in broad terms, are to be the characteristics of educational television as the Commission sees them:

• Educational television is to be constructed on the firm foundation of strong and energetic local stations. The heart of the system is to be in the community. Initiative will lie there, the overwhelming proportion of programs will be produced in the stations, scheduling will be performed by the local station and staff. Local skills and crafts will be utilized and local talents tapped.

• Public Television, as one of the two principal components of educational television, is to be provided with such abundant programming as to offer for each local station both diversity and choice. Enough of this programming will come from major national production centers or from stations in the great metropolitan areas to assure that localism within the system will not become parochialism. Like a good metropolitan newspaper, the local station will reflect the entire nation and the world, while maintaining a firm grasp upon the nature and the needs of the people it serves.

The Corporation for Public Television will provide

for Public Television leadership, standards of excellence, and an instrument by which the hundreds of local stations can act from time to time in concert. It will itself be led by men and women of eminence and achievement, drawn from television, from allied fields, and from public life. The Corporation will serve the stations. It will exist primarily to make it possible for those stations, one by one, to provide the greatest possible service to their communities.

• Public Television is to be supported by revenues from a manufacturer's excise tax on television sets, beginning at $40 million a year and rising in time to $100 million a year, received by the Treasury and held in trust for the Corporation. The tax at the outset will be at the rate of 2 percent, and will rise in time to a ceiling of 5 percent — half the tax that was imposed on television sets a few years ago. The mechanism will permit federal funds to flow to Public Television outside the ordinary budgeting and appropriations procedures, and thus insulate the system from direct governmental overseeing of its day-to-day operations and from the danger of political interference with the substance of programming. Should funds from communications satellite operations flow to the system, they can be used to reduce the excise tax rate.

• Other costs to the system, such as the capital and basic operating costs of the local stations which support the substructures for both Public and instructional television, may ultimately bring the total annual cost to approximately $270 million a year. These further costs will be met by state and local governments, by the federal government acting through the Department of Health, Education, and Welfare, and by foundations and other private sources.

• Funds are to be provided without impinging upon the freedom of the stations, and without relieving the community of its obligation to support its station. Federal funds used to support the production of programs will be disbursed in a fashion that minimizes any risk that the substance of those programs will be affected by political or governmental involvement. The stations themselves will produce most of the programs, and will have at all times freedom in deciding whether any program is to be broadcast. That freedom is made real because funds will be adequate to provide alternatives, for freedom is scarcely present when the choice lies between the program that is supplied or nothing at all.

• A stimulus to art and technology will be brought into being from which the rewards are incalculable. In every major city in the United States there will be a television station operating with funds commensurate with its needs, and likely to be receptive to the writer, the producer, the director, the performer, or the artist who believes he has something to contribute to the culture or the perception of his fellow citizens. There will be room for the young man and woman in a developing stage, for the experimenter, the dissenter, the visionary. The innovator will be able to try his art without being subject to the tyranny of the ratings.

• Support services, for which until now there has been no place, will be organized and provided. Interconnection will for the first time enable Public Television to bring to all the people of the United States those events of great national importance or interest which now go unreported until they have passed. But there will also be the less obvious services: the training programs, the provision of archives, the development of new technology, which until now have not existed at all or have been supported only where they promise immediate commercial advantage.

• Institutional arrangements are provided that can be responsive to the great changes in technology and the use of television that we see ahead. Papers by Professor Albert G. Hill and Professor Joseph C. R. Licklider, published in the supplement to this Report, provide some glimpses and suggestions of future changes and opportunities which educational television will be prepared to evaluate and when appropriate to bring into use for the benefit of the home television audience of the future.

• The educators will possess, for the first time, powerful instruments in strong, well-supported, well-equipped stations from which to launch new and greater efforts in formal and informal education. Station staffs, familiar at new levels with the intricacies of program production, can turn their new skills to the service of instruction. Universities, in concert with the large stations or with the national production centers, will be able to embark upon the profound study which is required before television can be fully comprehended as a tool of education, and will be able to proceed to the creation of pilot programs which absorb the best uses of television into the full variety of educational tools.

There will be, in sum, an enterprise in being from which all Americans can take heart.

The Road Ahead

Such a system will not spring into full-bodied being at one time. There must be a long period of recruitment, during which many more men and women of talent and devotion are attracted to the new enterprise. There must be an even longer period in which the system can grow, slowly and perhaps haltingly, to its full stature. It is, after all, a system that depends upon the ideas of those fallible humans who make it up; ideas do not come easily, nor are all of them likely to be good.

Finally, there is no manner in which the system can be imposed upon a state or municipality. The Corporation exists to create opportunity. Where there is an inclination to move forward with the Corporation, no barriers intervene. Where a state system or local station prefers to go its own way, it can certainly do so; the assistance it may wish to seek from the Department of Health, Education, and Welfare is in no way prejudiced, nor is it to be prevented from making any other appeal for funds it may find suitable. In all cases, the station will have available to it the programs emanating from the system, to use or ignore as it sees fit.

Programs: The Test of the System

Its programs will constitute the test of the system: programs developed at the national centers, programs produced by the stations themselves, programs of a pioneering nature produced through the research centers. Whatever the institutional arrangements, however funds are secured, whatever the technologies that may be involved, the picture on the screen and the sounds that accompany it are what the viewer perceives; programs are the measure of what the system accomplishes. It is in terms of its programs that Public Television promises a wider vision and a better utilization of television's power to enlarge the life of every citizen.

The institutional arrangements we have proposed have as their central purpose making available to Public Television the funds, the facilities, the personnel, and the environment which are essential for first-rate programming. Public Television will be able to pioneer with program substance, with talent, with format. In this lies its true promise.

The major innovation in Public Television will arise out of the environment it will provide to attract talented people and release their skills and creativity in a medium of great service to the American public. This environment, with its freedom, its scope, and its adequate facilities, should enable Public Television to develop a broad range of quality programs beyond anything now available.

The task of programming will require facilities equal to the objectives of Public Television. There must be adequate studios, color equipment, interconnection. Public Television must be able to bring orchestra and opera groups and dance groups into its own studios. Local stations must have mobile equipment to permit them to go outside the studios and to interpret the active life of their communities. For the challenge of programming to be met, Public Television must have, in far greater numbers than now available, people with skill, imagination, and devotion. It must be able to offer compensation sufficient to attract highly able people. It must have the time to take pains and be creative. It must be able to establish a climate of inventiveness, experimentation, and enterprise. It must have the means to make its promise real.

In discussing the programming potential of educational

television, there is always a temptation to promise or to expect too much too quickly. To achieve the quality of programming that we hope for will take time. We are aware of how difficult it is for commercial television, with its immense resources, to achieve great programs. In Public Television there will be failures, and at times it may seem that its failures are more evident than its successes; but we believe that the institutional arrangements we have proposed will point Public Television in directions that will lead ultimately into more substance and quality in programs. Miracles cannot be expected overnight, but we are convinced that the curve of quality in Public Television will be steadily upward.

Fulfilling the Promise

With difficulties realistically in mind, and with an acute awareness of the hazards inherent in discussing illustrative examples drawn from a program field as wide in scope and diverse in possibility as that of Public Television, we offer the following general observations with regard to the opportunities that will exist for Public Television programming.

Public Television programming can deepen a sense of community in local life. It should show us our community as it really is. It should be a forum for debate and controversy. It should bring into the home meetings, now generally untelevised, where major public decisions are hammered out, and occasions where people of the community express their hopes, their protests, their enthusiasms, and their will. It should provide a voice for groups in the community that may otherwise be unheard.

Public Television programs can help us see America whole, in all its diversity. To a degree unequaled by any other medium, Public Television should be a mirror of the American style. It should remind us of our heritage and enliven our traditions. Its programs should draw on the full range of emotion and mood, from the comic to the tragic, that we know in American life. It should help us look at our achievements and difficulties, at our conflicts and agreements, at our problems, and at the far reach of our possibilities. Public Television programs should help us know what it is to be many in one, to have growing maturity in our sense of ourselves as a people.

Public Television can increase our understanding of the world, of other nations and cultures, of the whole commonwealth of man. Public Television programs should keep pace, in their attention to world affairs, with the revolutionary technology that is making every part of the world instantaneously accessible to every other part. Through Public Television programs, and through advances in the technology of communication, Americans should have rapidly increasing opportunities for greater insight into the nature of other nations and cultures, for a clearer understanding of struggles and settlements between nations, for a view far beyond our own borders into the ways of the rest of the world. Public Television programs should take us into other traditions, should expose us to other histories, should let us see how we and the world look from other vantage points on the globe, and should let us reflect on the quiet achievements, raging crises, and the joys and pains of ordinary life elsewhere in the world.

Public Television can open a wide door to greater expression and cultural richness for creative individuals and important audiences. It should seek out able people whose talents might otherwise not be known and shared. The search for new or unrecognized ability should include but not be limited to conventional ideas of talent. There should be a search for the unusual, for the commonplace skill uncommonly mastered, for the rare personality, for the familiar expressing itself in new ways.

Public Television programs should show us domains of learning, emotion, and doing, examples of skill, human expressiveness, and physical phenomena that might otherwise be outside our ken. It should bring to us new knowledge and skills, lifting our sights, providing us with relaxation and recreation, and bringing before us glimpses of greatness. Public Television programs should have the means to be daring, to break away from narrow convention, to be human and earthy. Public Television programming should explore new dimensions of artistic performance not ordinarily available to our nation's audiences. It should present important playwrights whose work is too seldom performed. It should give a stage to experimental drama, to the work of promising young playwrights in search of an audience. It should provide a vehicle for the best of the yet unknown actors and actresses, a concert stage for unknown but talented musical artists. It should encourage and use films that display vital originality. It should promote further experimentation in choreography, pantomime, music, drama, lighting, staging, and all aspects of artistic and dramatic presentation in terms of television. Without lowering its aims, Public Television can be marked by exuberance or naturalness or simplicity, reaching for the things that make the world kin, that join together reality and delight.

Public Television can be powerfully educational, even when it is not presenting formal instruction. Public Television programs should carry the best of knowledge and wisdom directly into the home. Great teachers should have opportunities to interpret the new math, the new physics, the new social sciences through home television. Some of the best educational films of the past decade were made as teaching aids to new curricula. They should be adapted to television.

The unique opportunity is to bring before those who seek to understand, those who understand deeply. Public Television should give each home the opportunity to be a center for learning, where knowledge and scholarship are informally and expertly available. Public Television has already demonstrated its capacity to be responsive to the people's hunger for knowledge and self-improvement, but it is only at the threshold of what might be done.

Programs for Children

Important as this can be for adults, the informal educational potential of Public Television is greatest of all for children. The powerful impact of television upon children is known to every parent in the land. Public Television programs should give great attention to the informal educational needs of preschool children, particularly to interest and help children whose intellectual and cultural preparation might otherwise be less than adequate. For schoolchildren in their home hours, Public Television programs should provide a wealth of exposure to the variety of information and experiences a really educated person gets outside of formal instruction. Programs should help extend a child's powers of observation and expression; they should increase his "visual literacy" about the meaning of objects and processes; they should heighten his natural curiosity; they should open up a world of visual reality, linking it to a comprehension of the abstract, the metaphorical, and the imaginary.

Public Television's responsibility for informal education, of adults as well as children, is of a high order, requiring sensitivity to the natural pleasure most children and adults anticipate when they go to the television set. Programs to meet this responsibility will require art forms beyond that of most formal teaching, and will utilize adventure, surprise, suspense, and humor as their tools.

Contemporary Affairs

Public Television can extend our knowledge and understanding of contemporary affairs. Its programming of the news should grow to encompass both facts and meaning, both information and interpretation. It should be historian, in addition to being daily journalist. Its programs should call upon the intellectual resources of the nation to give perspective and depth to interpretation of the news, in addition to coverage of news day by day. This enlarged canvas should show us the interplay of people and events, in terms of time and place, history and consequence. Programming in contemporary affairs should be sensitive to the long groundswells of civilization as well as to its earthquakes.

Public Television's programs should search out the influences that different fields have on each other, looking at the relationships between science and politics, art and therapy, technology and agriculture, psychology and warfare, outer space and international relations. Programs should assess the broad significance of a news item: the mine disaster, the Supreme Court decision, the new tax, the labor strike, the scientific discovery. The bare reporting of incidents is not sufficient to meet the responsibilities we see for Public Television. Programs should find ways to show us the context of incidents, the past and present from which they spring, the impact they may make on tomorrow.

Analysis of Ideas

Public Television can serve Americans by providing analysis of much more than the events of current history. Just as there is a scarcity of thorough analysis and interpretation of the news, there is an even greater scarcity of television analysis of forms and ideas in art and philosophy, in music and literature, in science and technology, and in other fields of human expression and endeavor. With rare exceptions, such analysis as one finds is limited to the narrow confines of the panel discussion, the interview, or the formal lecture. Much greater imaginativeness and inventiveness are needed in programming for the analysis of forms and ideas. Public Television programs should be much more than a crude public stage for such presentation. With freedom and imagination, Public Television programming should be an innovative laboratory for the analysis of the intellectual, artistic, and social substance of our culture.

Encouraging Spontaneity

Public Television can realize, much more fully than television does now, the spontaneous, the live, the flexible qualities of which the medium is capable. Most television today is rigidly planned and executed. There should be, in addition, the wide latitude, the great magic that television has for giving us a window on the instant, for letting us be *there* when something is happening. Public Television should give attention to programming the unpredictable, the sudden events and unique occasions where actions and reactions are not known in advance, where there is suspense, excitement, and the actuality of life.

Flexibility of Scheduling

Public Television programs, in addition, should have a flexibility of scheduling which is now ordinarily denied the medium. Television is, among other things, a narrative medium which functions within and against a flow of time. Here, as in the poem, the play, the symphony, man seeks to give humanly significant form to the irrepressible flow of time. Currently, stifling restrictions are imposed upon artistic and imaginative freedom in television by the necessity to shape aesthetic forms and program content and length to economic considerations. The conventional rigid approach to scheduling, while appropriate to commercial television where modules of time have a market value, should not be permitted to dominate Public Television. Instead, Public Television programming should free the creative artist and technician to explore the full uses of the medium, allowing them to give priority to the aesthetic motive, to the moral and intellectual quest.

Encouraging Innovation

Public Television can encourage innovation, experimentation, and improvement in programming by incentives built into the Corporation's grants to stations and production centers. Special incentives should be used to spur the development of innovative ideas and forms for new and neglected areas of programming. In addition to the usual grants made for financing program production, incentives should be supplied to give particular encouragement to innovation in program content and method, opening up fields and techniques not ordinarily dealt with.

The Sense of History

Public Television, finally, has significant, unexploited opportunities to serve an important historical function in conserving the best of the medium's programs. The system, including the Corporation we have proposed, should encourage the development of archives, especially for the purpose of preserving the best of Public Television's own programs. The great debates in public life, the crucial hearings, the great performances, moments of national tragedy and triumph, the living presence of men and women who should be known to generations ahead, are examples of what such archives should preserve for the future. At present, television is an insatiable user of program material. It is likely to continue to be so in the future. Most of its materials are used only for a brief time, and then they are lost. Much of the best as well as the worst is erased or destroyed; in consequence, television today wastes much of value that we cannot possibly replace. We are convinced that Public Television has a responsibility of the first order to conserve as well as to create, to provide a selective preservation of the best of its contributions to man's life and art.

The Faith to Be Free

The Commission cannot decline to recognize that there is involved in the acceptance of its proposal a great act of faith. Public Television, in the end, will stand or fall on its ability to attract men and women — artists, technicians, managers, leaders — of high skill and high devotion. Without such persons, the effort will create little of worth, however ample the funds and however sound the organization. The Commission has that faith. Public Television can offer people of talent and ideas a magnificent new opportunity to share what they have to share, and in so doing, to grow in their own powers. We believe that Public Television can aspire to a freedom and excellence which will persuade creative people that it is a medium through which they can best express themselves.

If we were to sum up our proposal with all the brevity at our command, we would say that what we recommend is freedom. We seek freedom from the constraints, however necessary in their context, of commercial television. We seek for educational television freedom from the pressures of inadequate funds. We seek for the artist, the technician, the journalist, the scholar, and the public servant freedom to create, freedom to innovate, freedom to be heard in this most far-reaching medium. We seek for the citizen freedom to view, to see programs that the present system, by its incompleteness, denies him.

Because this freedom is its principal burden, we submit our Report with confidence: to rally the American people in the name of freedom is to ask no more of them than they have always been willing to provide.

Acknowledgments

During the course of the study, the Commission invited many people to appear at its meetings in order to consult directly with experts in the numerous areas of the Commission's concerns. Their names, and their affiliations at the time of their association with the work of the Commission, follow.

Those who counseled with the Commission were: James Armsey, the Ford Foundation; Robert Bates, the Rockefeller Brothers Fund; William Benton, Encyclopaedia Britannica; McGeorge Bundy, the Ford Foundation; John W. Bystrom, Department of Health, Education, and Welfare; Everett Case, Alfred P. Sloan Foundation; Douglass Cater, the White House; Joseph V. Charyk, Communications Satellite Corporation; Wilbur J. Cohen, Department of Health, Education, and Welfare; John F. Dille, Jr., National Association of Broadcasters; C. Scott Fletcher, National Association of Educational Broadcasters; Robert L. Foreman, Popular Science Publishing Company, Inc.; Lee E. Franks, Georgia State Department of Education; Lewis Freedman, WNDT, New York, New York; Fred W. Friendly, the Ford Foundation; John W. Gardner, Department of Health, Education, and Welfare; Hartford N. Gunn, Jr., WGBH, Boston, Massachusetts; William G. Harley, National Association of Educational Broadcasters; Leland Hazard, Pittsburgh Plate Glass Company; E. William Henry, Federal Communications Commission; Harold Howe II, Department of Health, Education, and Welfare; Joseph D. Hughes, the Richard King Mellon Foundation; Devereux C. Josephs, New York Life Insurance Company; Francis Keppel, Department of Health, Education, and Welfare; John W. Kiermaier, WNDT, New York, New York; Winston E. Kock, National Aeronautics and Space Administration; Norman Lloyd, the Rockefeller Foundation; James Loper, KCET, Los Angeles, California; Ralph Lowell, Boston Safe Deposit and Trust Company; Warren G. Magnuson, United States Senate; Leonard Marks, United States Information Agency; Jack McBride, KUON–TV, Lincoln, Nebraska; William J. McCarter, WETA–TV, Washington, D.C.; James McCormack, Jr., Communications Satellite Corporation;

Donald H. McGannon, Westinghouse Broadcasting Company; Paul A. Miller, Department of Health, Education, and Welfare; J. D. O'Connell, Director of Telecommunications Management; Edward Purcell, Harvard University; James Robertson, KCET–TV, Los Angeles, California; John C. Schwarzwalder, KTCA–TV, Minneapolis, Minnesota; Frank Stanton, Columbia Broadcasting System; Roger L. Stevens, National Foundation for the Arts and the Humanities; David C. Stewart, National Foundation for the Arts and the Humanities; Donald V. Taverner, WQED–WQEX, Pittsburgh, Pennsylvania; Sylvester L. Weaver, Jr., Subscription Television, Inc.; John F. White, National Educational Television; Jerome Wiesner, Massachusetts Institute of Technology; Arnold J. Zurcher, the Alfred P. Sloan Foundation.

The Commission wishes to thank the following people who prepared background papers or other materials which were invaluable in making this report: Lillian Ambrosino; Martin Codel, television consultant; Edwin G. Cohen, National Center for School and College Television; John Crosby, the *Observer*, London; James Day, KQED–TV, San Francisco, California; Benjamin DeMott, Amherst College; Wilson P. Dizard; Ronald Gross, Academy for Educational Development, Inc.; Richard D. Heffner, Rutgers University; Edward Herlihy, Radio Corporation of America; Arthur Hungerford, Pennsylvania State University; Louis L. Jaffe, Harvard University; Warren A. Kraetzer, WHYY, WUHY, Philadelphia, Pennsylvania; Joseph C. R. Licklider, Massachusetts Institute of Technology; Judith Murphy, Academy for Educational Development, Inc.; Frank Orme, National Association for Better Broadcasting; Edward J. Pfister, National Center for School and College Television; Donald R. Quayle, Eastern Educational Network; Robert F. Schenkkan, KLRN–TV, San Antonio–Austin, Texas; Otto F. Schlaak, WMVS, WMVT, Milwaukee, Wisconsin; Wilbur Schramm, Stanford University; Crocker Snow, Jr., WGBH–FM, Boston, Massachusetts; Sydney Sowles; Arthur E. Sutherland, Harvard University; John W. Taylor, WTTW, WXXW, Chicago, Illinois; E. B. White, the *New Yorker*.

The Commission wishes to thank the following people who served on panels convened by the Commission: L. G. Abraham, Bell Telephone Laboratories; Clifford J. Benfield, Columbia Broadcasting System; Kurt Borchardt, House Committee on Interstate and Foreign Commerce, and Harvard University; Louis G. Cowan, Columbia University; John P. Cunningham, Cunningham & Walsh, Inc.; Lawrence T. Frymire, Television Advisory Committee, State of California; Peter Goldmark, CBS Laboratories; C. J. Hirsch, Radio Corporation of America; Roy Huggins, Universal City Television Studios; Richard B. Hull, WOSU–TV, Ohio State University; Carl Kaysen, Harvard University; Paul W. MacAvoy, Massachusetts Institute of Technology; Mark Massel, the Brookings Institution; James Meyer, Educational Services Incorporated; M. S. Novik, radio consultant; Barney Oliver, Hewlett-Packard; Charles A. Siepmann, New York University; Sam J. Slate, RKO General Broadcasting; Harold E. Wigren, National Education Association; Nicholas Zapple, Senate Committee on Commerce.

The Commissioners and staff have also profited from consultations with and the suggestions of: Kenneth Adam, British Broadcasting Corporation; David C. Adams, National Broadcasting Company; Rustan Älveby, Sveriges Radio; Frank W. Anderson, Jr., National Aeronautics and Space Administration; Gerard L. Appy, National Educational Television; David Attenborough, British Broadcasting Corporation; Carlo Baldi, Radiotelevisione Italiana; Claude Barrere, International Radio and Television Society; Luigi Barzini, author; Edwin R. Bayley, National Educational Television; Michel Beilis, American Telephone and Telegraph Company; Richard H. Bell, National Association of Educational Broadcasters; Virginia Biggy, Eastern Educational Network; Gary B. Bisson, Smithsonian Institution; David Blank, Columbia Broadcasting System; A. William Bluem, Syracuse University; John Boesel, A. C. Nielsen Company; Fred Boud, Granada TV Centre; Frank Bowles, the Ford Foundation; Frederick Breitenfeld, Jr., National Association of Educational Broadcasters; Leon Brooks, Columbia Broadcasting System; Robert Cassmeier, National Broadcasting Company; Henry J. Cauthen, South Carolina ETV Network; Marcus Cohn, Cohn and Marks; J. Michael Collins, WNED–TV, Buffalo, New York; Joan Ganz Cooney, WNDT, New York; Bernarr Cooper, New York State Department of Education; John Coplin, Department of the Treasury; Claes Dahlgren, Swedish Broadcasting Corporation; S. F. Damkroger, American Telephone and Telegraph Company; Roy Danish, Television Information Office; Curtis W. Davis, National Educational Television; Howard R. Dressner, the Ford Foundation; Daniel Emerson, American Telephone and Telegraph Company; Everett H. Erlich, American Broadcasting Company; Thomas E. Ervin, National Broadcasting Company; Alvin

Eurich, Institute for Humanistic Studies; Hans Geert Falkenberg, Westdeutscher Rundfunk; John Fischer, *Harper's Magazine;* Franklin Fisher, Massachusetts Institute of Technology; John Frantz, Department of Health, Education, and Welfare; Henry Geller, Federal Communications Commission; Hugh Gillis, Boston University; Ben Gilmer, American Telephone and Telegraph Company; Erwin Griswold, Harvard University; Albert R. Gurney, Jr., Massachusetts Institute of Technology; Robert Hilliard, Federal Communications Commission; Raymond Hurlbert, Alabama Educational Television Commission; Father Neil Hurley, Catholic University, Santiago, Chile; Rosel H. Hyde, Federal Communications Commission; Nicholas Johnson, Federal Communications Commission; Pierre Juneau, Board of Broadcast Governors, Canada; Benjamin Kaplan, Harvard University; Walter J. Kelly, American Telephone and Telegraph Company; C. A. Killner, American Research Bureau; William Kobin, National Educational Television; Hubert L. Kurtz, American Telephone and Telegraph Company; Eric Larrabee, *Horizon;* William B. Lodge, Columbia Broadcasting System; Jack Ludwig, Hughes Aircraft Company; Rolf Lundgren, Sveriges Radio; Howard Mandel, National Association of Broadcasters; Chalmers H. Marquis, National Association of Educational Broadcasters; James G. Miller, EDUCOM; Paul A. Miller, Department of Health, Education, and Welfare; Newton N. Minow, Leibman, Williams, Bennett, Baird and Minow; Lucian Neitzel, Norddeutscher Rundfunk; Italo Neri, Radiotelevisione Italiana; Kenneth E. Oberholtzer, Denver Public Schools; A. C. Ocker, American Telephone and Telegraph Company; Carl F. J. Overhage, Massachusetts Institute of Technology; Marguerite Owen, Tennessee Valley Authority; McIvor L. Parker, Federal Communications Commission; Finlay Payne, Canadian Broadcasting Corporation; Michael Peacock, British Broadcasting Corporation; Ithiel de Sola Pool, Massachusetts Institute of Technology; Birgit de Radwan, Sveriges Radio; Henry Rahmel, A. C. Nielsen Company; Marshall Robinson, the Ford Foundation; Winfried Scharlau, Norddeutscher Rundfunk; Arthur Schatzow, Federal Communications Commission; Robert C. Seamans, Jr., National Aeronautics and Space Administration; Joseph E. Slater, the Ford Foundation; Walter D. Sohier, National Aeronautics and Space Administration; Raymond J. Stanley, Department of Health, Education, and Welfare; Julius A. Stratton, the Ford Foundation; Herta Sturm, Zweites Deutsches Fernsehen; Beverly Taylor, Federal Communications Commission; Gordon Thayer, American Telephone and Telegraph Company; James E. Webb, National Aeronautics and Space Administration; Gerhardt Wiebe, Boston University; Robert Williamson, National Aeronautics and Space Administration; Ken Winslow, Western Radio and Television Association; Franz Wordemann, Westdeutscher Rundfunk.

The Commission is appreciative of the contributions to the study by the correspondents involved in the detailed survey of educational television stations throughout the United States. They are: Norton Bloom, television director, writer; George E. Condon, *Cleveland Plain Dealer;* Lawrence Laurent, *Washington Post;* Alan Levy, freelance writer; Leo Litwak, author, teacher; Al McConagha, *Minneapolis Tribune;* Sylvan Meyer, *Daily Times,* Gainesville, Georgia; Warner Twyford, *Virginian-Pilot;* Lawrence G. Weiss, *Denver Post.*

Operating Educational Television Stations
as of December 1966

Map No.		Channel	
MAINE			
1 Presque Isle	WMEM–TV	10	University of Maine
2 Calais	WMED–TV	13	University of Maine
3 Orono	WMEB–TV	12	University of Maine
4 Augusta	WCBB	10	Colby-Bates-Bowdoin Educational Television Corporation
NEW HAMPSHIRE			
5 Durham	WENH–TV	11	University of New Hampshire
MASSACHUSETTS			
6 Boston	WGBH–TV	2	WGBH Educational Foundation
NEW YORK			
7 Rochester	WXXI	21	Rochester Area Educational Television Association
8 Buffalo	WNED–TV	17	Western New York Educational Television Association, Inc.
9 Syracuse (Liverpool)	WCNY	24	Educational Television Council of Central New York
10 Schenectady	WMHT	17	Mohawk-Hudson Council on Educational Television, Inc.
11 New York	WNYC–TV	31	City of New York, Municipal Broadcasting System
12 New York	WNDT	13	Educational Broadcasting Corporation
CONNECTICUT			
13 Hartford	WEDH	24	Connecticut Educational Television Corporation
PENNSYLVANIA			
14 Pittsburgh	WQED	13	Metropolitan Pittsburgh Educational Television
	WQEX	16	
15 University Park	WPSX–TV	3	The Pennsylvania State University
16 Scranton	WVIA	64	Northeastern Pennsylvania Educational Television
17 Hershey	WITF–TV	33	South Central Educational Broadcasting Council
18 Bethlehem (Allentown)	WLVT–TV	39	Lehigh Valley Educational Television Corporation
19 Philadelphia	WUHY–TV	35	WHYY, Inc.
DELAWARE			
19 Wilmington (See Phila.)	WHYY	12	WHYY, Inc.

Map No.			Channel	

DISTRICT OF COLUMBIA

20	Washington	WETA–TV	26	The Greater Washington Educational Television Association, Incorporated

VIRGINIA

21	Richmond	WCVE–TV	23	Central Virginia Educational Television Corporation
22	Hampton–Norfolk	WHRO–TV	15	Hampton Roads Educational Television Association

NORTH CAROLINA

23	Chapel Hill	WUNC–TV	4	University of North Carolina
24	Charlotte	WTVI	42	Charlotte-Mecklenburg Board of Education
25	Columbia	WUNB–TV	2	University of North Carolina

SOUTH CAROLINA

26	Greenville	WNTV	29	South Carolina Educational Television Commission
27	Columbia	WRLK	35	South Carolina Educational Television Commission
28	Charleston	WITV	7	South Carolina Educational Television Commission

GEORGIA

29	Athens	WGTV	8	Regents of the University System of Georgia for and on behalf of the University of Georgia
30	Wrens	WCES–TV	20	Georgia State Department of Education
31	Atlanta	WETV	30	Board of Education, City of Atlanta
32	Columbus–Warm Springs	WJSP–TV	28	Georgia State Department of Education
33	Savannah	WVAN–TV	9	Georgia State Department of Education
34	Waycross	WXGA–TV	8	Georgia State Department of Education

FLORIDA

35	Jacksonville	WJCT	7	Community Television, Inc.
36	Tallahassee	WFSU–TV	11	The Board of Regents of the State of Florida for and on behalf of Florida State University
37	Gainesville	WUFT	5	Board of Regents, acting for and on behalf of the University of Florida
38	Orlando	WMFE–TV	24	Florida Central East Coast Educational Television, Inc.
39	Tampa	WUSF	16	The State Board of Regents of Florida, a Public Corporation of the State of Florida, acting for and on behalf of University of South Florida

Map No.		Channel	
40	Tampa– St. Petersburg	WEDU	3	Florida West Coast Educational Television, Inc.
41	Miami	WSEC–TV WTHS–TV	17 2	The Board of Public Instruction of Dade County, Florida

ALABAMA

42	Huntsville	WHIQ	25	Alabama Educational Television Commission
43	Birmingham	WBIQ	10	Alabama Educational Television Commission
44	Mt. Cheaha State Park	WCIQ	7	Alabama Educational Television Commission
45	Montgomery	WAIQ	26	Alabama Educational Television Commission
46	Dozier	WDIQ	2	Alabama Educational Television Commission
47	Mobile	WEIQ	42	Alabama Educational Television Commission

LOUISIANA

48	New Orleans	WYES–TV	8	Greater New Orleans Educational Television Foundation

OHIO

49	Toledo	WGTE	30	The Greater Toledo Educational Television Foundation
50	Cleveland	WVIZ–TV	25	Educational Television Association of Metropolitan Cleveland
51	Bowling Green	WBGU–TV	70	Bowling Green State University
52	Newark	WGSF	28	Newark Public School District, Newark, Ohio
53	Columbus	WOSU–TV	34	The Ohio State University
54	Oxford	WMUB–TV	14	The President and Trustees of the Miami University
55	Cincinnati	WCET	48	The Greater Cincinnati Television Educational Foundation
56	Athens	WOUB–TV	20	Ohio University

KENTUCKY

57	Louisville	WFPK–TV	15	Board of Trustees, Louisville Free Public Library

TENNESSEE

58	Nashville	WDCN–TV	2	Metropolitan Board of Education
59	Memphis	WKNO–TV	10	Memphis Community Television Foundation

MICHIGAN

60	University Center	WUCM–TV	19	Delta College
61	East Lansing	WMSB	10	Board of Trustees, Michigan State University
62	Detroit	WTVS	56	Detroit Educational Television Foundation

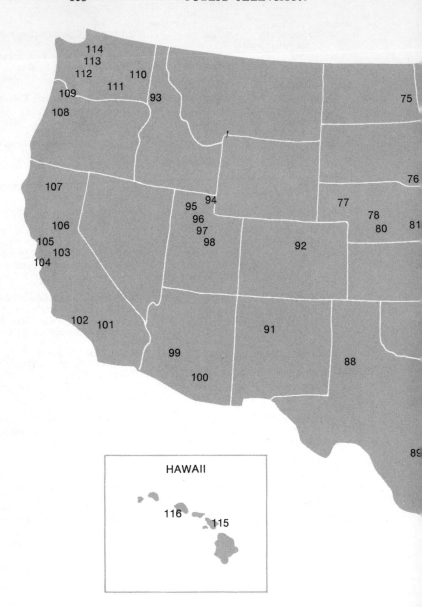

PRESENT SYSTEM

Map No.		Channel	

WISCONSIN

63	Milwaukee	WMVS	10	Board of Vocational and Adult Education
		WMVT	36	Board of Vocational and Adult Education
64	Madison	WHA–TV	21	The Regents of the University of Wisconsin

MINNESOTA

65	Duluth–Superior, Wisconsin	WDSE–TV	8	Duluth-Superior Area Educational Television Corporation
66	St. Paul– Minneapolis	KTCA–TV	2	Twin City Area Educational Television Corporation
		KTCI–TV	17	
67	Appleton	KWCM–TV	10	Twin City Area Educational Television Corporation

IOWA

| 68 | Des Moines | KDPS–TV | 11 | Des Moines Independent Community School District |

ILLINOIS

69	Chicago	WTTW	11	Chicago Educational Television Association
		WXXW	20	
70	Urbana	WILL–TV	12	University of Illinois Board of Trustees
71	Carbondale	WSIU–TV	8	Board of Trustees, Southern Illinois University

MISSOURI

| 72 | Kansas City | KCSD–TV | 19 | School District of Kansas City, Missouri |
| 73 | St. Louis | KETC | 9 | St. Louis Educational Television Commission |

ARKANSAS

| 74 | Little Rock | KETS | 2 | State of Arkansas Educational Television Commission |

NORTH DAKOTA

| 75 | Fargo | KFME | 13 | North Central Educational Television Association, Inc. |

SOUTH DAKOTA

| 76 | Vermillion | KUSD–TV | 2 | University of South Dakota |

NEBRASKA

77	Alliance	KTNE	13	Nebraska Educational Television Commission
78	North Platte	KPNE–TV	9	Nebraska Educational Television Commission
79	Omaha	KYNE–TV	26	Nebraska Educational Television Commission
80	Lexington	KLNE–TV	3	Nebraska Educational Television Commission
81	Lincoln	KUON–TV	12	The Board of Regents of the University of Nebraska

Map No.			Channel	
KANSAS				
82	Topeka	KTWU	11	Washburn University of Topeka
OKLAHOMA				
83	Tulsa	KOED–TV	11	The Oklahoma Educational Television Authority
84	Oklahoma City	KOKH–TV	25	Oklahoma City Public Schools
85	Oklahoma City	KETA–TV	13	The Oklahoma Educational Television Authority
TEXAS				
86	Richardson	KRET–TV	23	Richardson Independent School District
87	Dallas	KERA	13	Area Educational Television Foundation, Inc.
88	Lubbock	KTXT–TV	5	Texas Technological College
89	Austin– San Antonio	KLRN	9	Southwest Texas Educational Television Council
90	Houston	KUHT	8	University of Houston
NEW MEXICO				
91	Albuquerque	KNME–TV	5	Regents of the University of New Mexico and the Board of Education of the City of Albuquerque, New Mexico
COLORADO				
92	Denver	KRMA–TV	6	Denver Public Schools
IDAHO				
93	Moscow	KUID–TV	12	University of Idaho
UTAH				
94	Logan	KUSU–TV	12	Utah State University of Agriculture and Applied Science
95	Ogden	KOET	9	Ogden City Schools
96	Ogden	KWCS	18	Weber County School District
97	Salt Lake City	KUED	7	University of Utah, Board of Regents
98	Provo	KBYU–TV	11	Brigham Young University
ARIZONA				
99	Phoenix	KAET	8	Arizona Board of Regents for Arizona State University
100	Tucson	KUAT	6	
CALIFORNIA				
101	San Bernardino	KVCR–TV	24	San Bernardino Valley Joint Union Junior College District
102	Los Angeles	KCET	28	Community Television of Southern California
103	San Jose	KTEH	54	Santa Clara County Office of Education
104	San Mateo	KCSM–TV	14	San Mateo Junior College District
105	San Francisco	KQED	9	Bay Area Educational Television Association

Map No.		Channel	
106 Sacramento	KVIE	6	Central California Educational Television
107 Redding	KIXE	9	Northern California Educational Television
108 OREGON			
109 Corvallis	KOAC–TV	7	Oregon State Board of Higher
Portland	KOAP–TV	10	Education
WASHINGTON			
110 Pullman	KWSC–TV	10	Washington State University
111 Yakima	KYVE	47	Yakima County School District
112 Lakewood Center	KPEC–TV	56	Clover Park School District 400
113 Tacoma	KTPS	62	Tacoma School District 10
114 Seattle	KCTS–TV	9	The University of Washington
HAWAII			
115 Wailuku	KMEB	10	University of Hawaii
116 Honolulu	KHET	11	
PUERTO RICO			
117 Hato Rey (San Juan)	WIPR–TV	6	Department of Education of Puerto Rico
118 Mayaguez	WIPM–TV	3	

NOTE: In addition, KBZK operates in Pago Pago, American Samoa, and connects with six relay stations.

Supplementary Papers

The papers that follow were prepared for the use of the Commission, and are presented here for their general interest or reference value.* Each is signed by its author. The views expressed are those of the authors, and not necessarily those of the Commission, whose own views and judgments are expressed solely in the Report of the Carnegie Commission on Educational Television, which precedes these papers. In addition to these essays, the supplement includes selected statistical material on educational television which was prepared by or for the Commission.

*Dr. Licklider's paper was completed after the Commission had formulated its own conclusions.

MEMORANDUM OF LAW
Various Legal Aspects of the Corporation for Public Television

by Ernest W. Jennes

Mr. Jennes is a graduate of the Yale Law School (L.L.B., 1942) and a Member of the Bar of the District of Columbia.

The Carnegie Commission on Educational Television proposes the establishment of a nonprofit nongovernmental corporation chartered by or under an act of Congress. The Corporation, although expected to receive and disburse private, state, and local government funds, would principally be financed through federal funds. The affairs of the Corporation would be governed by a board of directors comprised of twelve persons who would serve for six-year terms. Six members of the board would be appointed by the President of the United States with the concurrence of the Senate. After the initial six appointments two such appointments would be made every two years. The remaining six members of the board would initially be elected by the first six appointed members. Thereafter, two members would be elected every two years by the entire board. It is contemplated that the membership of the board would be chosen to provide a broad representation of various regions of the country, various professions and occupations, and various kinds of talent and experience appropriate to the functions and responsibilities of the Corporation.

Although established to carry out policies defined by the Congress as being in the broad public interest, the Corporation would not be an agency or establishment of the United States and neither it nor its officers or employees would be subject to federal laws governing agencies or establishments of the United States, except to the extent the statute establishing the Corporation might specifically provide. The basic source of federal funds for the Corporation would be a manufacturer's excise tax on television receivers. Amounts equal to the proceeds of this tax, net of refunds, would be paid into a trust fund maintained in the Treasury of the United States. Money would be disbursed from the trust fund and paid directly to the Corporation without the necessity of further action by the Congress or the executive branch of the government except for transfer of the funds.

The Carnegie Commission has selected such an organization and manner of federal financing because it has been mindful of the long-standing American tradition of fostering the expression of ideas and the communication of information free from government control or oversight; the desirability of maximizing experimentation, innovation, and freedom for creativity in programming; the sensitivity of the relationship between the government and the content of television programs, and the importance of minimizing the involvement of the government in this general area.

The basic purpose of the Corporation would be to attempt to extend and improve noninstructional educational television, which is described in the Carnegie Commission's Report as "Public Television." Public Television relates essentially to programs intended for the general viewer rather than for use in classrooms or for which some kind of academic credit may otherwise be earned.

The following functions of the Corporation have been considered in analyzing the legal questions discussed in this Memorandum:

1. The procurement of programs from various independent contractors for national distribution to participating noncommercial educational television stations.

2. The provision of financial support for the establishment or expansion of centers for the production of Public Television programming for national distribution, the provision of financial support to strengthen the capacity of a limited number of local noncommercial educational broad-

cast stations for the production of programs of more than local interest, and, in both situations, the making of grants or contracts for programs.

3. The establishing and maintaining of a system of interconnection which, although providing some "live networking," would be used primarily as a means of distribution of programs. In either case the individual broadcast station would have sole discretion to determine whether a particular program should be broadcast and, if so, the time of broadcast.

4. Helping to support the production of local Public Television programming by noncommercial educational television stations for broadcast to meet the needs of the particular community or area served by the stations.

Although the Carnegie Commission's Report does not spell out in full detail the relationship between the proposed Corporation and the various program producers with which it would be doing business, it is apparent that in the normal course of events the new Corporation would have to exercise numerous judgments and make frequent selections in the programming area. These activities would principally include decisions regarding the general types of programs for which it would contract. The activities could also relate to whether particular programs would be produced and distributed nationally and certainly would relate to whether particular programs would be available on a "live network" basis. These activities would necessarily be performed in the light of program content and of standards of quality. Moreover, the Corporation could arrange for terminations when the programs did not meet quality standards. In short, the Corporation would inevitably make a wide range of programming decisions. Since it is anticipated that the programs to be developed would include news in depth, comment on important public issues, and the like, programs produced under contract with the Corporation would not infrequently involve controversial issues, but every effort would be made to assure a balanced presentation of positions and attitudes.

It is basic to the Carnegie Commission's proposal that although each participating noncommercial educational television broadcast station would have available the total programming provided by the Corporation for national distribution, each station alone would determine whether to broadcast the program at all, whether to broadcast it live or at such other time as it chooses and how many times to broadcast the same program. This approach is far more than an effort to meet technical legal requirements as to broadcast station responsibility; it is intended to assure that the fundamental public policies favoring local and area voices in many communities in this country, through television broadcast stations attuned to local and area needs and providing service to the entire local and area public, will not be undermined by undue centralization.

Our views have been asked with respect to the following legal questions:

1. Whether the Congress may provide for the establishment of a nongovernmental corporation such as is proposed here and entrust it with the accomplishing of public purposes.

2. Whether federal funds may be made available to the Corporation in the manner proposed.

3. Whether the nongovernmental nature of the Corporation and the proposed method of financing would give the Corporation the flexibility the Carnegie Commission seeks.

4. Whether the activities of the Corporation which have been described above would abridge the First Amendment guarantees of free speech and free press.

1. THE CONGRESS MAY PROVIDE FOR THE ESTABLISHMENT OF A NONGOVERNMENTAL CORPORATION SUCH AS IS PROPOSED HERE AND ENTRUST IT WITH THE ACCOMPLISHING OF PUBLIC PURPOSES.

Numerous corporations and other organizations relevant to the proposal of the Carnegie Commission on Educational Television have been chartered or otherwise established by or under an act of Congress.[1] These include a variety of patriotic, service, and educational organizations,[2] and some private commercial enterprises such as the Union Pacific Railroad[3] and, most recently, the Communications Satellite Corporation (COMSAT).[4] Among them are the Daughters of the American Revolution,[5] the American Legion,[6] the Boy Scouts of America,[7] the Future Farmers of America[8] and the Civil War Centennial Commission, which planned and prepared the program to commemorate the one hundredth anniversary of the Civil War.[9] Another such corporation is the Civil Air Patrol, which serves as a private civilian auxiliary to the United States Air Force.[10] The American National Red Cross is a federally chartered private corporation which has long been entrusted with important public responsibilities.[11]

Three organizations of special interest are the National Academy of Sciences,[12] Howard University,[13] and the Smithsonian Institution.[14] The National Academy of Sciences is a federally chartered nongovernmental organization which may be called upon by the government to "investigate, examine, experiment and report on any subject of science or art. . . ."[15] Howard University is a private corporation, with a self-perpetuating board of trustees, which is fed-

[1] Some forty-eight organizations, including some of those discussed in the text, are listed in the 1964 Act to Provide for Audit of Accounts of Private Corporations Established under Federal Law. Annual audits by independent accountants are required and the report of the audit is submitted to the Congress. 36 U.S.C.A. §§ 1101–03 (Supp. 1965).

[2] See 36 U.S.C. (1964).

[3] Act of July 1, 1862, ch. 120, 12 Stat. 489.

[4] 47 U.S.C. § 701–44 (1964).

[5] 36 U.S.C. §§ 18–18b (1964).

[6] 36 U.S.C. §§ 41–51 (1964).

[7] 36 U.S.C. §§ 21–29 (1964).

[8] 36 U.S.C. §§ 271–91 (1964).

[9] 36 U.S.C. §§ 741–49 (1964).

[10] 10 U.S.C. § 9441 (1964); 36 U.S.C. §§ 201–08 (1964).

[11] 36 U.S.C. §§ 1–16 (1964).

[12] 36 U.S.C. §§ 251–54 (1964).

[13] 20 U.S.C. §§ 121–29 (1964).

[14] 20 U.S.C. §§ 41–84 (1964).

[15] 36 U.S.C. § 253 (1964).

erally chartered.[16] The Smithsonian Institution performs a large number of public responsibilities although it is a federally chartered nongovernmental corporation.[17] These include a wide range of educational and cultural activities, among which are the operation of national museums and art galleries,[18] the performance of broad scientific research activities,[19] and the operations of the National Zoological Park,[20] the John F. Kennedy Center for the Performing Arts,[21] and the International Exchange Service.[22] Other illustrations are the American Historical Association, charged with the improvement of the condition of historical study;[23] the National Fund for Medical Education,[24] which, among other things, promotes methods and techniques of medical education; the National Safety Council, which has an important role in promoting methods of safety, protection and health of the citizens of the United States;[25] and the Foundation of the Federal Bar Association, which improves and promotes the administration of justice, including means of handling the legal business of the federal departments and establishments.[26]

We have already referred to COMSAT, a private commercial entity which was established under an act of Congress to effect a public purpose. COMSAT was made possible by preexisting appropriations of massive amounts of public moneys which had been expended in research and development for satellite communications. Communication by space satellite is of vital importance to national interests and national policies and a matter of direct governmental

[16] Act of March 2, 1867, ch. 162, 14 Stat. 438; 20 U.S.C. §§ 121–29 (1964).

[17] 20 U.S.C. § 41 (1964).

[18] See, e.g., 20 U.S.C. §§ 50, 59, 71, 76, 77 (1964).

[19] See, e.g., 20 U.S.C. §§ 78, 79–79b (1964).

[20] 20 U.S.C. §§ 81–84 (1964).

[21] Act of September 2, 1958, 72 Stat. 1698, amended by 73 Stat. 573 (1959), amended by 77 Stat. 128 (1963), amended by 78 Stat. 4 (1964).

[22] See 20 U.S.C. § 49 (1964).

[23] 36 U.S.C. § 20 (1964).

[24] 36 U.S.C. §§ 601–17 (1964).

[25] 36 U.S.C. §§ 461–79 (1964).

[26] 36 U.S.C. §§ 571–89 (1964).

concern. Nonetheless, in view of the tradition of private ownership of the nation's communications system, a plan was developed to allow the vigor inherent in our nongovernmental system to be devoted to the development of communications by space satellites for the benefit of all the people.[27] The parallel between what was done in the case of satellite communications and the present case is very relevant. There a resource was created at public expense and "given" to a private entity, which has been charged with furthering the development of that resource. In the present case, the Corporation will have the similar function of continuing the development and expansion of noncommercial educational television.

It may be concluded, therefore, that there is nothing unusual or improper in a proposal that the Congress designate a federally chartered, nongovernmental, nonprofit corporation to play a major role in the advancement of noncommercial educational television. Rather, such a proposal is consistent with a long line of precedents.

2. FEDERAL FUNDS MAY BE MADE AVAILABLE TO THE CORPORATION AND THIS MAY BE DONE IN THE MANNER PROPOSED.

Most of the private organizations discussed above have been provided with resources from the federal government. Sometimes these resources have taken the form of the use of buildings or other facilities[28] and sometimes the form of equipment and supplies or aid of government personnel,[29] but frequently the federal government has directly provided funds.[30] For present purposes, the critical point is not the nature of the particular resource that has been provided but the marriage of the federal government and private persons or institutions to accomplish public purposes which has been part of the American tradition from the turning

[27] See H.R. Rep. No. 1636, 87th Cong., 2d Sess. 7–8 (1962).
[28] 10 U.S.C. § 2602 (1964) (American National Red Cross).
[29] See 10 U.S.C. § 9441 (1964) (Civil Air Patrol); 36 U.S.C. § 288 (1964) (Future Farmers of America).
[30] See, e.g., 20 U.S.C. § 123 (1964) (Howard University); 20 U.S.C. § 101 (1964) (American Printing House for the Blind).

over of public land on the frontier to veterans of the Revolutionary War, through the land grants which made possible the building of the great transcontinental railroads, and up through the establishment of COMSAT.

In considering the proposal to provide the Corporation federal funds by establishing a manufacturer's excise tax on television receivers, it is important to note that, under the Constitution, the Congress has wide discretion in determining how it will appropriate funds.[31] Most appropriations to government agencies are in the form of annual legislation. However, appropriations to government agencies may have carryover provisions;[32] they may be for a period of years in specified sums, or they may be for a period of years according to some formula.[33] They may be for lump sums without detailed specification of particular uses.[34] Moreover, the Congress has used a number of different techniques for earmarking federal revenues for various purposes and has used other techniques to eliminate the need for annual appropriations in whole or in part.

Such techniques have included blanket allocation of revenues generated by, or capital funds raised by, the entity in question. Thus the Tennessee Valley Authority, although obtaining some of its moneys through annual appropriations like other government agencies, has two other important sources of funds — (1) revenues generated from the sale of power and various products and (2) the sale of electric power bonds.[35] Annual appropriations are used to finance the operating expenses and capital expenditures of the nonpower operations and capital expenditures of the power operations.[36] Even within its annual appropri-

[31] Save only in the case of the two-year limitation on military appropriations to be found in Article 1, Section 8, Clause 12, of the Constitution.

[32] See Land and Water Conservation Act of 1965, § 3, 78 Stat. 899 (1964).

[33] See Land and Water Conservation Act of 1965, § 4(b), 78 Stat. 900 (1964).

[34] See Jones, *The Financing of TVA*, 26 Law & Contemp. Prob. 725 (1961).

[35] *Id.* at 726.

[36] *Id.* at 730.

ation financing the Congress has provided TVA with substantial flexibility. Most appropriations are granted as lump sums and, in addition, there are normally no fiscal-year limitations on the use of the funds. So, too, the St. Lawrence Seaway Development Corporation has been provided with similar authority to use its revenues from the operation of the Seaway without further specific appropriation.[37] Another illustration is Federal Prison Industries, Inc., a government corporation which provides employment and vocational training for prison inmates and generates its own revenues through the sale of products manufactured by prisoners to government departments and agencies.[38]

The Congress has also provided for trust or similar funds, financed by taxes, into which the proceeds of a tax are paid, or amounts equal to its proceeds are credited to an account and held in the Treasury for use in carrying out specified purposes or programs as provided by statute. Familiar illustrations are the Old Age and Survivors Insurance Trust Fund,[39] the Disability Insurance Trust Fund,[40] and the Railroad Retirement Account.[41] Funds are disbursed under the terms of the basic legislation, which provides both the source of the trust fund and the authority to spend it. In the case of the Migratory Bird Conservation Fund, the Congress has authorized a permanent appropriation from a fund made up from the fees on federal hunting licenses.[42] Expenditures from the fund are not subject to annual appropriation but rather are made according to a statutory formula, which allocates the funds for various purposes.[43] Another illustration is the Wildlife Restoration Fund, in which excise taxes on firearms and ammunition have been permanently appropriated to the Department of the Interior and paid into a special fund from which moneys

[37] 33 U.S.C. § 984(a)(12), (b) (1964).
[38] 18 U.S.C. §§ 4122, 4124, 4126 (1964).
[39] 42 U.S.C. § 401 (1964).
[40] *Ibid.*
[41] 45 U.S.C. § 228o (1964).
[42] 16 U.S.C. § 718d (1964).
[43] See 16 U.S.C. § 718d (a)–(c) (1964).

are disbursed to the states for wildlife restoration.[44] There are other similar earmarked taxes or customs duties used in conjunction with permanent appropriations or special funds, thus obviating the need for annual appropriations.[45]

We have seen, therefore, that the Congress adapts the method of providing federal funds to the needs of the situation. There remain three questions: (1) Is the purpose for which sums equal to excise tax receipts would be put into a trust fund a constitutionally proper governmental purpose? (2) Does it make any difference that the funds would be paid over to a nongovernmental corporation rather than a government agency or establishment? (3) Would there be an unconstitutional delegation of legislative power to a private organization?

First, as to the validity of the basic purpose — development and expansion of educational television throughout the United States — it seems beyond reasonable question, especially in the light of the long history of federal support of cultural and educational activity and the more recent broad federal support of educational activity generally, that the purpose is constitutionally proper. In this connection it should be noted that the validity of the purpose of a congressional appropriation (*e.g.*, whether it is for the "general welfare") and the terms and conditions which the Congress places on the use of the appropriation are ones as to which the Congress has wide discretion.[46]

---

[44] Annual appropriation authorized by Act of September 2, 1937, ch. 899, § 3, 50 Stat. 917. Appropriation made permanent by the General Appropriation Act of 1951, ch. 896, 64 Stat. 693 (1950).

[45] An amount equal to the proceeds of the excise tax on sport fishing tackle is available in the form of a general fund to the Department of the Interior through permanent appropriations for grants to states for fish restoration and management. The appropriation was authorized by the Act of August 9, 1950, ch. 658, § 3, 64 Stat. 431, and made permanent by the Interior Department Appropriation Act of 1952, 65 Stat. 262 (1951). All customs duties collected in Puerto Rico are paid to the government of Puerto Rico from a trust fund. 48 U.S.C. § 740 (1964).

[46] See, *e.g.*, Spaulding v. Douglas Aircraft Co., 60 F. Supp. 985 (S.D. Calif. 1945), *aff'd*, 154 F.2d 419 (9th Cir. 1946); Kansas Gas & Elec. Co. v. Independence, Kansas, 79 F.2d 32 (10th Cir. 1935). The courts have even suggested that such an issue may present a political

Second, in our judgment the propriety of the proposal would not be affected by the fact that the moneys are to be disbursed to a nongovernmental body rather than a governmental body. As previously indicated, there is nothing new about accomplishing public purposes through private entities. Appropriations of funds are made to the National Academy of Sciences, a federally chartered but nongovernmental corporation.[47] Substantial annual appropriations are made to Howard University, another federally chartered corporation.[48] Substantial federal funds have long been appropriated to the Smithsonian Institution.[49] There is a fund originally created from appropriations and retained in the Treasury the income of which the Secretary of the Treasury is required by statute to pay directly to the American Legion for the maintenance and perpetuation of Pershing Hall in Paris.[50] Similarly, for many years there has been a trust fund the income of which has been paid to the American Printing House for the Blind, a private philanthropic corporation chartered under Kentucky law, for the purpose of printing books for general distribution to the blind.[51]

The argument might be made that the particular manner in which the Carnegie Commission proposes that the Corporation be financed would significantly differentiate it from the numerous instances described above in which the Congress has chosen to accomplish public purposes through private means. Thus, it might be contended that even though there is a long tradition of disbursing public funds to nongovernmental institutions and well-established prece-

---

question, impinging on the constitutional separation of powers. See United Biscuit Co. v. Wirtz, 359 F.2d 206 (D.C. Cir.), *cert. denied,* 384 U.S. 971 (1966); Spaulding v. Douglas Aircraft Co., *supra.* One court has stated, "moreover, it would seem impossible in this connection for a court to establish workable criteria by which to distinguish those acts of Congress which created valid appropriations from those which did not." United Biscuit Co. v. Wirtz, *supra* at 213 n. 14.

[47] 36 U.S.C. § 253 (1964).
[48] 20 U.S.C. § 123 (1964).
[49] See, *e.g.,* 20 U.S.C. §§ 53a, 70, 75g (1964).
[50] 36 U.S.C. § 491 (1964).
[51] 20 U.S.C. § 101–05 (1964).

dent for earmarking of public funds, including tax revenues, for specified purposes, nonetheless there is no precise precedent for earmarking tax revenues for disbursement to a private entity. However, we find nothing in the combination of these two features which diminishes the force of the precedent behind each of them separately so as to render the result improper.[52]

Third, there is the question whether the use by the Congress of a private corporation to accomplish public purposes, when combined with the provision of federal funds, would amount to an unconstitutional delegation of legislative power to a private organization. We think the answer is no.

There is a long line of authority that the Congress may properly delegate to private organizations functions which it could either perform itself or authorize a governmental agency to perform. Thus, for example, in *St. Louis, Iron Mountain & Southern Ry. Co.* v. *Taylor,* 210 U.S. 281, 287 (1908), the Supreme Court upheld, as a valid delegation, legislation directing the American Railway Association, a private trade association, to fix uniform height standards for railroad cars used in interstate commerce.[53] *Carter* v. *Carter Coal Co.,* 298 U.S. 238 (1936), does not cause us to conclude that any different result is required here. There the Supreme Court found the Bituminous Coal Act of 1935 to be unconstitutional. The statute, the Court held, improperly delegated the power to fix wages and hours in the coal industry, since the wages and hours limitations

[52] Conceivably an attack upon the tax might be made on the ground that it represented a taking of property without due process by reason of the fact that the proceeds of the tax were disbursed to a private entity. The closest analogy we have been able to find is in Dayton-Goose Creek Ry. Co. v. United States, 263 U.S. 456 (1924), where a due process challenge was made to the validity of the "recapture" provisions of the Transportation Act of 1920, which provided for the payment of "excess profits" of railroads into a fund for the support of weaker railroads to enable them "more effectively to discharge their public duties." *Id.* at 484. Despite the fact that the levy challenged was for the benefit of competitors of the parties bringing the challenge, the Supreme Court unanimously upheld its constitutionality.

[53] See also Buttfield v. Stranahan, 192 U.S. 470 (1904).

would be adopted by a two-thirds vote of the private coal producers. The Court stated that the statutory procedure was legislative delegation in its most obnoxious form, because it gave this power to private persons "whose interests may be and often are adverse to the interests of others in the same business." [54]

Since the *Carter Coal* case, there has been a consistent judicial disinclination to hold congressional delegations unconstitutional, whether to private groups or administrative agencies.[55] In the subsequent cases involving legislative delegation to private groups the courts have upheld the delegation and distinguished *Carter Coal. Currin v. Wallace,* 306 U.S. 1 (1939), upheld an act of Congress that gave the Secretary of Agriculture authority to designate tobacco grades and standards and auction markets in which tobacco moves in interstate commerce. The statute provided that the Secretary could not designate such a market unless two-thirds of the tobacco growers in the area voted for such designation. The Court distinguished *Carter Coal* as a case in which a private group made law and forced it on a minority of its competitors.[56]

The courts, in this area, usually state that the delegation will be proper provided the Congress has set out some standard that the delegatee may use to guide the exercise of its judgment.[57] This "standards" approach applies whether the delegation is to private bodies or to administrative agencies.[58] It should be noted, however, that standards need not be set out in detail; rather they may be stated in very general terms.[59] The Supreme Court in *Yakus* v.

[54] Carter v. Carter Coal Co., 298 U.S. 238, 311 (1936).

[55] See 1 DAVIS, ADMINISTRATIVE LAW § 2.14 (1958).

[56] Currin v. Wallace, 306 U.S. 1, 15–16 (1939).

[57] Sunshine Anthracite Coal Co. v. Adkins, 310 U.S. 381 (1940); United States v. Rock Royal Co-op., 307 U.S. 533 (1939).

[58] See, *e.g.,* 1 DAVIS, ADMINISTRATIVE LAW § 2.14 (1958); Note, *Delegation of Power to Private Parties,* 37 Colum. L. Rev. 447, 461 (1937); *cf.* Sunshine Anthracite Coal Co. v. Adkins, *supra* note 57; United States v. Rock Royal Co-op., *supra* note 57.

[59] See 1 DAVIS, ADMINISTRATIVE LAW § 2.03 (1958) for examples of such standards.

United States, 321 U.S. 414, 425 (1944), stated the following broad test to determine the adequacy of a standard:

> whether the definition sufficiently marks the field within which the Administrator is to act so that it may be known whether he has kept within it in compliance with the legislative will.

It may be concluded that *Carter Coal* turned on an issue which is not presented by the proposal of the Carnegie Commission and that the force of *Carter Coal* itself has been seriously weakened since it was decided. It seems clear that, with properly drafted legislation, the Congress could set forth a sufficient degree of guidance for the Corporation so that there would not be an unconstitutional delegation of the Congress's power to legislate. Such a statute would state the purposes for which the Corporation is to be created and "the field within which [it] is to act" and either the legislation or its congressional history would presumably contain findings that the purposes underlying the statute are in the public interest, that they are deemed appropriate for congressional action and that large federal funds are required but it is in the further public interest to insulate the government as much as possible from the activities which the Corporation is intended to carry out.

An attempt might be made to argue that the particular details of the proposal render the conventional precedents on congressional delegation of power inapplicable. We see nothing in the combination of earmarked taxes with a non-governmental recipient entity which raises problems of delegation of power. The earmarking of tax revenues does not represent an abdication of congressional power to dispose of public resources, since the Congress could at any time simply repeal or amend the authorizing legislation. Indeed, the use of earmarked taxes without annual appropriation represents less of a disposition of ultimate governmental power over the public resources involved than does the outright appropriation of capital resources for the use of private entities, which has ample precedent.

3. THE NATURE OF THE CORPORATION AND METHOD OF FINANCING WOULD GIVE THE CORPORATION THE FLEXIBILITY THE CARNEGIE COMMISSION SEEKS.

The Carnegie Commission's Report contemplates that the Corporation would have the attributes of a typical private nonprofit corporation, enjoying the usual advantages and subject to the ordinary limitations of such a corporation. This could readily be achieved by appropriate provision in the authorizing legislation specifying that the Corporation was to be treated as a private entity and not as a governmental agency or establishment.

One primary advantage is the managerial flexibility provided by the corporate format. The board of directors would have the necessary authority to govern the internal affairs and activities of the Corporation. An extremely important power would be to provide for the hiring (and firing) of officers, agents, and employees at such terms, salaries, and other benefits as it finds necessary to accomplish the Corporation's purpose. In this way the board of directors would be in a position to select appropriate individuals and permit them the desirable freedom to work toward the objectives and purposes for which the Corporation is to be created. As a private entity, the Corporation would be free from the personnel requirements of civil service and the classification laws which normally apply to governmental departments, agencies and establishments.

The Corporation would also have a desirable degree of independence from the government in conducting its fiscal affairs. It would be free from the close budgeting review by the Bureau of the Budget and other agencies of the executive branch which normally applies to government bodies but which might have a deadening effect in the area of creativity. It would also be free from auditing by the General Accounting Office, which carries with it the power of the Comptroller General to settle and adjust the books of the agency, although, of course, its affairs would be subject to regular independent audit. As a private nonprofit corporation, the Corporation would also be free from other governmental procedural and administrative regulations that could impair its effectiveness in developing programming. For example, the Corporation could negotiate contracts without public advertisement and competitive bidding.

Its affirmative powers would be those of any nonprofit, private corporation and would include the power to sue or be sued in its own name; to enter into contracts and make grants; to invest or lend its funds; to borrow money; to publish a journal; to hold all real and personal property wherever located, whether acquired by sale, lease, gift, or in any other manner; and, in general, to have all powers that are necessary and proper to extend and improve a noncommercial educational television service. The Corporation would be able to acquire or merge into itself other nonprofit, private corporations upon its own initiative.

In addition, the fact that the Corporation would be nonprofit and organized for educational purposes would mean that it would be able to qualify as a tax-exempt organization entitled to receive tax-deductible contributions under the Internal Revenue Code. This in turn would provide it access to important sources of funds which would help maintain its independence.

4. THE PROPOSED ACTIVITIES OF THE CORPORATION DO NOT ABRIDGE THE FIRST AMENDMENT GUARANTEES OF FREE SPEECH AND FREE PRESS

The final question[60] to be considered is whether the proposed activities of the Corporation would constitute an abridgment of freedom of press or speech under the First Amendment.[61]

It must be recognized at the outset that the First Amend-

[60] We have not considered the issue whether there would be legal standing to raise such a question, cf. Massachusetts v. Mellon and Frothingham v. Mellon, 262 U.S. 447 (1923), since the Carnegie Commission wishes its proposals to be within the bounds of the First Amendment in any event.

[61] It is now established that the First Amendment relates to radio and television. See, e.g., Joseph Burstyn, Inc. v. Wilson, 343 U.S. 495 (1952); United States v. Paramount Pictures, Inc., 334 U.S. 131, 166 (1948); Superior Films v. Department of Educ., 346 U.S. 588 (1954) (concurring opinion).

ment is concerned with the activities of the government and government instrumentalities, not with those of private entities as such.[62] The Carnegie Commission's proposal contemplates creation of a corporation, specifically intended to be treated for all legal purposes as a private entity and not as an agency or establishment of the United States. The mere fact that a corporation is chartered or authorized by the federal government does not make it a government instrumentality for purposes of First Amendment applicability.[63] Of course, a nongovernmental corporation may be held to be a governmental instrumentality for some constitutional purposes and still retain its private character.[64] There is, however, a good possibility that for First Amendment purposes the Corporation would be considered a nongovernmental entity; and, if this were so, the question of the applicability of the First Amendment to its activities would not arise.[65]

[62] See, e.g., Public Util. Comm'n v. Pollak, 343 U.S. 451, 461 (1952); McIntire v. William Penn Broadcasting Co., 151 F.2d 597, 601 (3d Cir. 1945), cert. denied, 327 U.S. 779 (1946); Reiter v. American Legion, 189 Misc. 1053, 72 N.Y.S.2d 345 (Sup. Ct.), aff'd, 273 App. Div. 757, 75 N.Y.S.2d 530 (1947).

[63] See Public Util. Comm'n v. Pollak, supra note 62; Reiter v. American Legion, supra note 62.

[64] For example, the entity may be so closely related to governmental activity as to be held immune from state taxation. In Department of Employment v. United States, 35 U.S.L. Week 4052 (U.S. Dec. 12, 1966), the Court stated, "on the merits, we hold that the Red Cross is an instrumentality of the United States *for purposes of immunity from state taxation levied on its operations . . .*" Ibid. (emphasis added).

[65] The Carnegie Commission's proposal would not present a case in which an ostensibly private organization is a sham, see Smith v. Allwright, 321 U.S. 649 (1944); United States v. Classic, 313 U.S. 299 (1941); or in which it is the government, no matter what it is called, see Evans v. Newton, 382 U.S. 296 (1966); Marsh v. Alabama, 326 U.S. 501 (1946). Under current Supreme Court decisions, it does not appear that the Corporation would be found to have a degree of governmental involvement or control sufficient to render it a government instrumentality for First Amendment purposes. See Public Util. Comm'n v. Pollak, 343 U.S. 451 (1952); cf. Burton v. Wilmington Parking Authority, 365 U.S. 715 (1961) (equal protection clause — Fourteenth Amendment); but cf. Kerr v. Enoch Pratt Free Library, 149 F.2d 212 (4th Cir. 1945) (equal protection clause — Fourteenth Amendment); Griffin v. State Bd. of Educ., 239 F.

Even if the Corporation were held to be a governmental instrumentality in the constitutional sense, we do not believe that the activities in which it is intended to engage would abridge the First Amendment. For purposes of analysis under the First Amendment, the most sensitive types of activities proposed for the Corporation are the acquisition of programming for national distribution and the arranging for interconnection of stations so that those programs can be distributed nationally.

The program acquisition activities of the Corporation might be challenged on the theory that, by the inevitable process of selection and rejection of programs, the Corporation would place impermissible limitations on the freedom of expression of the program producers. But the courts have been concerned when the government has acted to inhibit the free expression of ideas. As far as can be determined, the courts have not found affirmative efforts to develop and expand various forms of communications to be an abridgment, even when the government itself does so. Such efforts have included strictly governmental reports and press releases; books, films, and radio programs prepared by or for the United States Information Agency, and creative and artistic works supported by the writers, artists, and theater projects of the Works Progress Administration in the 1930's, and, more recently, by the National Foundation for the Arts and the Humanities.

It might also be asserted that, as to the program producer whose work is rejected, the Corporation would inhibit freedom of speech by denying a government benefit, causing an impermissible prior restraint on speech. This ground is also without merit. There would be no penalty involved in rejecting a producer's work.[66] Programs found not acceptable for support by the Corporation would not be suppressed. They would be available for dissemination through other means. The situation would be unlike the cases in-

Supp. 560 (E.D. Va. 1965) (three-judge district court) (equal protection clause — Fourteenth Amendment).

[66] See Superior Films v. Department of Educ., 346 U.S. 587, 588 (per curiam) (Douglas, J., concurring).

volving use of the public mail or use of the second-class mailing permit where there was no other reasonably acceptable alternative.[67] In any event, to argue that the Corporation must support all programming or none would mean that the government itself could never hold out any grant, scholarship, subsidy, or other benefit to a private person on a selective basis. The government is not constitutionally compelled to support all enterprise — commercial and philosophical — or none at all.[68]

A question might also be raised as to the proposal that the Corporation establish and maintain an interconnection system for the distribution of the programs it procures to local stations. The First Amendment rights of free speech and free press include the protection of an effective means for disseminating and receiving communications.[69] The question presented is essentially a variation of the one just discussed. It warrants emphasizing, however, that the proposed activity would not destroy or limit the public's right to pick and choose among competing offerings.[70] Rather, the Commission seeks to expand, not contract, the channels of communications by providing new, additional, and diverse offerings of education, culture, information, entertainment, and other types of expression. The proposal is intended to stimulate rather than diminish free speech. The Corporation is intended to help provide the public with a greater selection of programs for home viewing. Moreover, the principal purpose of interconnection would be efficient distribution and not simultaneous broadcast by

[67] See, e.g., Hannegan v. Esquire, Inc., 327 U.S. 146 (1946); Ablard & Harrison, *The Post Office and the Publishers' Purse-strings: A Study of the Second-Class Mailing Permit*, 30 Geo. Wash. L. Rev. 567 (1962); Sigler, *Freedom of the Mails: A Developing Right*, 54 Geo. L.J. 30 (1965).

[68] See Hannegan v. Esquire, Inc., *supra* note 67, at 160 (Frankfurter, J., concurring).

[69] See, e.g., Griswold v. Connecticut, 381 U.S. 479, 482 (1965); Lamont v. Postmaster General, 381 U.S. 301 (1965); *id.* at 308 (concurring opinion); *cf.* Kovacs v. Cooper, 336 U.S. 77 (1949); Saia v. New York, 334 U.S. 558 (1948).

[70] See, e.g., Hannegan v. Esquire, Inc., 327 U.S. 146 (1946); *cf.* Public Util. Comm'n v. Pollak, 343 U.S. 451, 468 (1952) (Douglas, J., dissenting).

all participating stations. In any event, the individual stations would have sole discretion to decide whether to broadcast a particular program and, if so, the time of broadcast. This discretion in the local station would doubtless, in turn, affect the decisions of the Corporation as to the type of programs it would attempt to support and distribute.

One central purpose of government rules and regulations concerning broadcasting has been to *avoid* practices which would tend to limit the growth of diverse sources and means of communications and deprive the public and the local stations of choice of programs.[71] The Carnegie Commission's proposal is intended to expand television broadcasting and to provide further means of disseminating ideas from diverse sources. It seeks to give wider, not narrower, range to the public's opportunity to select from competing communications in the marketplace of ideas — an opportunity that underlies the principles of free speech and free press embodied in the First Amendment.

Conclusion

It is our judgment that it would be proper and consistent with precedent for the President and the Congress to conclude that the highly sensitive nature of the functions necessary to carry out the proposal considered in this Memorandum requires the use of an independent private entity, that large amounts of federal funds should be made available to that entity, and that such funds should be provided to the private entity in a manner that will best assure the continuation of its independent nature as well as the maintenance of a relatively stable source of revenues. It is also our judgment that the proposal considered here is consistent with the letter and spirit of the First Amendment.

COVINGTON & BURLING

By: ERNEST W. JENNES

December 27, 1966

[71] See National Broadcasting Co. v. United States, 319 U.S. 190, 198–209 (1943).

Costs of a Nationwide
Educational Television System
by Sidney S. Alexander

Based on a study prepared by Arthur D. Little, Inc., Industrial Consultants

Dr. Alexander is Professor of Management and Economics, Massachusetts Institute of Technology and sometime Economic Adviser, Columbia Broadcasting System, Inc.

THE MODEL

In order to put the Commission's recommendations into financial perspective, estimates were made of the costs of the entire educational television system of the country between the present and that future time when the goals of the Commission can reasonably be assumed to be achieved. To this end, a conceptual model was constructed of a fully developed educational television system that would, in the long run, substantially embody the Commission's recommendations.

The model is offered not as forecast but as projection — not as what will happen but what could happen. Its purpose is to illuminate the financial problems of the formative years of the system, and to trace the interrelationships of its many parts. Many judgments had to be made of matters that it will be the responsibility of others to decide. This was done not to invade their prerogative but rather to explore their problems in the hopes of gaining such understanding as would make those problems easier. It would be bothersome to emphasize at every step that each assumption is no more than an assumption, that it is made to clarify the problem rather than to predict or dictate, so the point is here emphasized once and for all. What follows, then, is an attempt to understand the way the system might develop in response to the proposals of the Commission within the constraints of the environment.

The actual evolution of the nation's educational television system will depend, under the Commission's proposals, on the success of local initiative, with private, state, and federal support, in establishing stations and in building up programming capability. The following projections of the future costs of the system are based on the assumption that both local initiative and financial support will be forthcoming to achieve by 1980 an educational television system satisfying, to a reasonable extent, the goals set by the Commission.

Number of Stations and Their Coverage

The Commission proposes that educational television service be made available to the entire population of the United States so far as that is economically practical. It is estimated that about 337 television stations at full practical power[1] are required to give as nearly complete coverage of the population of the United States as is economically justified. These 337 stations would bring about 94 percent of the population of the United States within a B contour of at least one educational station and 68 percent within an A contour.[2]

The criterion of economic feasibility underlying this estimate is that an educational station, to be economically justified, must carry its signal at grade B level or better to at least 70,000 people not similarly served by any other station. An educational station was also assumed to be justified if it brought a grade A signal to a metropolitan area of population over 140,000, or to a state capital, which was not similarly served by any other educational station.

[1] Full practical power was taken to be the maximum allowed for VHF, and 1000 kw for UHF, both at 1000 feet antenna height.

[2] For this study, grade B contours were assumed to be circles of radii 56 and 68 miles for UHF and VHF respectively. Grade A contours were assumed to be circles of radii 27 and 38 miles respectively. Grade B service for an area is technically defined by the condition that satisfactory service is to be expected at least 90 percent of the time at 50 percent or more of the receiving locations. Grade A implies satisfactory service at least 90 percent of the time at 70 percent or more of the receiving locations. No account was taken of terrain.

In applying these criteria, population estimates for 1980 were used, on the assumption, in accord with the middle range of the official estimates, that by 1980 the population of the country will have increased by 40 percent over that of 1960. It was also assumed that this percentage increase would apply uniformly over the entire country.

An additional 43 stations, making 380 in all, were taken to be economically justified as "second" educational stations in large metropolitan areas to which the Federal Communications Commission has allocated a second educational channel. These stations, it is estimated, will bring a second educational service to over one third of the nation at an incremental expense of $3.6 million annually for operation and depreciation, one of the biggest bargains in television. It *is* such a bargain because all the other resources are already present, the programs already produced and the interconnection lines already operating, so that all that is necessary is to put up more transmitters, connect them to the system, and feed them from "mother" stations which can take on this task without significantly increasing their expenses. It is by no means certain that all the second stations will be operated in this modest way, but it is the expenses for this mode of operation of the second stations that have been included in the cost estimates.

It should be emphasized that this model does not necessarily include all of the stations which might be appropriate in the future. Other stations over and beyond those included in this model may be useful to the system and sought by educational organizations.

Hours of Service

Each station is conceived as broadcasting fourteen hours a day, from 9:00 in the morning to 11:00 at night, except on Sundays, when it broadcasts from noon to 11:00 P.M. The first eight hours of each weekday will normally carry instructional programs, while Public programming will predominate after 5:00 P.M. On weekends almost all programming will normally be Public rather than instructional. Each station is accordingly to be on the air about ninety-five hours a week, with up to forty hours of instructional broadcasting from 9:00 to 5:00 weekdays, and possibly another five hours a week of instructional programming for adults in the evenings, leaving about fifty hours of evening and weekend broadcasting per week for Public Television programs. The system is thus to be used jointly for both instructional and Public broadcasting, and a large part of its costs are therefore joint costs.

Program Sources

The Public programs to be broadcast by any station are to be obtained from its own productions, exchange programs from other stations, and programs produced for national distribution under the auspices of the Corporation for Public Television. The Commission has recommended that about thirty hours of programming for national distribution be produced weekly, about one hour of national programming per week by each of perhaps twenty large metropolitan stations, and ten hours a week by contract producers, possibly under arrangements similar to those currently operated by National Educational Television (NET). In addition to these national programs, each of 210 originating stations is assumed to produce from one to ten hours a week of local and regional programming. The remaining 170 stations are projected to have no originating facilities at all. They will simply repeat programs fed from the nearest originating stations, typically about one hundred miles away. Each of the 43 second stations is assumed to be similarly fed by the first station in its city.

A large station would, accordingly, be able each week to draw its programming from the thirty hours of national programming created that week, from a large nationally accessible library of previously produced programs, from its own ten hours of program production for that week, and from any number of programs produced by other stations throughout the country available to it on an exchange basis. A small station would rely less upon its own program production but would probably draw more programming from other stations, particularly from its larger neighbors, as well as from the national sources. Even in those metropolitan areas which are to have two educational television stations, their one hundred hours of Public Television broadcast time can advantageously be programmed from this supply, largely through the repetition of worthwhile programs. Educational programming can well stand repetition, and unlike commercial television broadcasters, Public Television broadcasters should offer the public more than one opportunity of seeing a worthwhile program.

Programming Capability

The Commission recognized the development of program production capability at the local stations as the very first task in its proposed program for improving the educational television system. It was therefore assumed that in a fully developed system embodying the goals of the Commission any standard metropolitan area[3] of the United States not served from a larger city would have at least one educational television station with *some* production capability. Of the 380 stations on the list, 201 qualified as originating stations by this criterion, and 9 more were assumed to attain program-originating capability because they serve the capitals of their respective states, even though their principal cities are not large enough to qualify as standard metropolitan areas.

The programming capability that any one of these 210 originating stations was assumed ultimately to attain depended on the size and the statewide importance of the principal metropolitan area served by the station, as indicated in Table 1. The largest metropolitan area in each of the forty-seven states that have metropolitan areas was presumed to attain by 1980 a station whose leading position in its state is proclaimed by its name of "flag station." Flag stations were also assumed to be attained by thirteen "secondary" metropolitan centers, not the largest in their re-

[3] A standard metropolitan area is defined by the Executive Office of the President, Bureau of the Budget, as a county or a group of contiguous counties which contains a city, or cluster of cities, of 50,000 inhabitants or more.

TABLE 1

STATION POPULATION PROJECTION BY TYPE OF PROGRAMMING CAPABILITY

Type of Station	Projection Criterion	Number Meeting Criterion	Number in Type Class
ORIGINATING STATIONS			210
Flag Stations (Key or Regular)			
Serving Leading Metropolitan Area in State[a]		47	
Serving Secondary Metropolitan Center in State, 1980 Population Over 1 Million, Not Served by Grade A Signal from Larger City		13	
Total, Flag Stations			60
Assumed to Become Key Stations		20	
Regular Flag Stations		40	
Standard Stations			
Serving Metropolitan area, 1980 Population over 300,000 but Less than 1 Million, not Served by Grade A Signal from Larger City		57	
Serving Leading City in State, 1960 Population Less than 50,000		3	
Serving State Capital, not Otherwise Qualified for Standard Station		15	
Total, Standard Stations			75
Basic Stations			
Serving Metropolitan Area, 1980 Population over 140,000 but Less than 300,000, Not Served by Grade A Signal from Larger City		66	
Serving Metropolitan Area, 1980 Population Less than 140,000, Not Served by Grade B Signal or Better from a Larger City		9	
Total, Basic Stations			75
REPEATER STATIONS			
Serving a 1980 Population Greater than 70,000, Not Qualifying under Above Criteria as an Originating Station			170
Total Number of Stations, Originating and Repeater			380

[a] Including District of Columbia.

Source: Economic and Industrial Consultants to the Commission

spective states, but each with an estimated 1980 population over 1 million, and not served by a grade A signal from a larger city, so as to make 60 flag stations in all.

Two types of flag stations were distinguished, regular and key respectively, as shown in Table 2. The station taken to be representative of a regular flag station has two large, well-equipped black-and-white studios and a small mobile unit, with two black-and-white image orthicon cameras, and a film production team. It is adequately equipped and staffed to produce about ten hours of programming a week for local and exchange use. Its own production capability is limited to black-and-white, but like all other originating stations in the system it is capable of broadcasting color programs from tape or film, or from a color signal originated elsewhere and communicated to the station by electronic interconnection. About $3.3 million in capital expenditures are required to build and equip a representative regular flag station and $1.2 million in annual operating costs to keep it going. With annual capital costs at $300,000, its total costs run about $1.5 million a year.

Of the 60 flag stations, 40 were assumed to be regular flag stations in 1980. These will henceforth be referred to simply as flag stations. The remaining 20 flag stations are assumed to qualify by 1980 as key stations, producing color programs for national distribution as well as for local and exchange use. They would achieve that status by demonstrating their programming capability to the Corporation for Public Television. They would presumably receive support from the Corporation in enlarging their production facilities and in converting from black-and-white to color production capability, so as to achieve an adequate basis for the production of national programs and of local and regional programs of exceptionally high quality.

The station taken as representative of the key stations has three color-equipped studios and a fully equipped color mobile unit. It can produce, on the average, an hour a week of national programming in addition to the ten hours a week of local and exchange programming production characteristic of all flag stations. Of course, the local and

TABLE 2

CHARACTERISTICS OF STATIONS BY TYPE

	Station Type				
	Key	**Flag**	**Standard**	**Basic**	**Repeater**
	(Flag)	(Regular)			
Number of Stations (1980)	20	40	75	75	170
Average Population Served in 1980 (millions)[a]	4.0	1.0	0.8	0.3	0.2
Characteristic Metropolitan Area Population in 1980 (millions)	3.0	Largest in State, or 1.2	0.6	0.2	b
Population Range of Metropolitan Areas 1980 (millions)	1.2–15.0	Up to 1.8	0.3–1.0	0.1–0.3	b
Program Originating Capacity (hrs/wk) National	1	0	0	0	0
Local and Exchange	10	10	5	1–1½	0
Employees (full-time)[c]	167	97	36	9	0
Studios Number	3	2	1	1	0
Square Footage (thousands)	10.0	8.8	2.8	1.2	0
Camera Chains (studio)	9 Color	7 B&W	3 B&W	2 B&W	0
	(millions of dollars)				
Capital Required	6.2	3.3	1.7	1.3	0.55
Annual Operating Costs	3.0	1.2	0.49	0.16	0.038
Annual Capital Costs	0.6	0.3	0.16	0.13	0.047
Total Costs per Year	3.6[d]	1.5	0.65	0.29	0.085

[a] Unduplicated.

[b] Does not serve a metropolitan area.

[c] Excluding engineers attendant at transmitter.

[d] Including the $1,560,000 costs to a key station, on the average, of its 52 hours of national programming a year supplied to the entire system through the Corporation for Public Television.

Sources: Economic and Industrial Consultants to the Commission

References: Employees, Table 19; Capital Required, Table 18; Annual Costs, Table 17

exchange programming of a key station can be expected to be more expertly produced than that of a regular flag station. Indeed, it is in recognition of its ability to produce programs of superior quality that a station is to be supported by the Corporation in acquiring the additional facilities appropriate to programs of this quality, facilities that make it into a key station.

The capital facilities of a typical key station cost about $6.2 million,[4] or about $3 million more than those of a regular flag station. This difference in capital requirements would presumably be supported by the Corporation for Public Television. The average annual operating costs of the representative key station are estimated to be $3.0 million, which, with annual depreciation charges of $0.6 million, brings its total annual costs to $3.6 million. About $1.6 million of this total is expected to be defrayed by payments, at the average rate of $30,000 per hour of programming produced, from the Corporation for Public Television for the fifty-two hours of national programming that each key station would, on the average, contribute annually to the national system under contract with the Corporation. The *net* costs of a key station are, accordingly, about $2.0 million a year, or one-third greater than those of a regular flag station.

While the 60 flag stations, regular and key together, serve areas with total 1980 population of about 120 million, averaging 2 million per station, there is a very wide variation in the number served per station, depending upon the density of the population of the state. The largest flag station will serve about 25 million people in 1980, the smallest about half a million. But a flag station can be thought of as serving not only the population within reach of its broadcast signal, but all the people of its state or cultural area. Its program productions, both Public and instructional, are characteristically destined for broadcast not only over its own transmitter but, in large part, over a statewide or multistate system. Its programming capability

---

[4] See Tables 17, 18, and 19 for the details of the capital facilities and personnel requirements of a key station.

therefore is to be justified by the area served by its programs, rather than by the area served by its transmitter. For this reason each state having a metropolitan area was assumed to have a flag station, even though in some states the flag station's transmitter would serve a population considerably smaller than that served by a smaller station in a more densely populated state.

A metropolitan area with population less than 1 million but over 300,000 in 1980, not served by a grade A signal from a larger city, was assumed to have, in the long run, a station of the type designated as standard. Fifty-seven metropolitan areas, whose average 1980 population is estimated at 600,000, qualified for a standard station under this criterion. Standard stations were also assumed to be attained by the leading city of any state if that city has a 1960 population of less than 50,000 and therefore does not qualify for a flag station; 3 standard stations were justified by this criterion. Finally, if the state capital of any state was not served by a grade A signal from a station otherwise qualified, it also was assumed to be served by a standard station; 15 stations in cities not otherwise qualified for a standard station qualified by this criterion. Altogether, 75 stations were projected to be in the standard class in the long run.

The representative standard station has one well-equipped studio, a very small mobile unit equipped with vidicon cameras, and a small film unit. It can produce about five hours of local and exchange programming a week. Its film and tape units and its interconnection enable it to broadcast in color, as well as in black-and-white, an almost unlimited amount of taped and filmed programs supplied in those forms. Its facilities are estimated to cost about $1.7 million, and its annual operating costs to run about $490,000. With annual capital costs of $160,000, its total costs per year are about $650,000.

A metropolitan area with 1980 population over 140,000 but less than 300,000 and not served by a grade A signal from a larger city was assumed to have a basic television station in the long run. So was a metropolitan area with

1980 population under 140,000, if not served by a signal of grade B or better from a larger city. There are 66 basic stations justified by the first criterion and 9 by the second, making 75 basic stations in all.

A basic station has a small studio with two black-and-white image orthicon cameras and a peak time station complement of just seven people: a general manager who doubles as program producer and director, his assistant and a secretary-bookkeeper, two engineers at the studio for camera work, tape and film operation, broadcast control and maintenance, and an all-purpose operations crew of two men. This count does not include the engineers, if any, attendant at the transmitter, nor the second shift and weekend replacements required for the two engineers if the station is to run ninety-five hours a week. A basic station can be expected to turn out about an hour or an hour and a half of its own programming weekly. It is equipped with two tape and two film units, one of each able to handle color. It can also broadcast a color signal received over cable or microwave from the rest of the system.

The facilities of the representative basic station cost about $1.3 million. Its annual operating costs of $160,000 and annual capital costs of $130,000 bring its total annual costs to $290,000.

A station serving neither a standard metropolitan area nor the leading or capital city of a state was presumed to be a repeater station. A repeater station is simply a transmitter capable of rebroadcasting on its assigned frequency a signal fed to it over the microwave system. All localities meeting the criteria for having a station, principally by virtue of being able to extend educational television service to more than 70,000 people not otherwise served, are assumed to attain a repeater station in the long run unless they qualify for an originating station. There are 170 repeater stations in the model.

The annual operating and capital costs of a repeater station, like those of any other transmitter, are about $85,000 a year (Table 14). If it is a UHF repeater, the costs run $83,000 a year, if a VHF $93,000.

The equipment and operating expenses of a VHF transmitter are, exclusive of the cost of attendant engineers, substantially lower than those of a UHF transmitter of nearly comparable coverage — $64,000 and $83,000 respectively. But FCC regulations require engineering attendance at a VHF but not at a UHF transmitter, which accounts for a $29,000 extra cost for attendance at a VHF transmitter (Table 14).

Interconnection

All the stations in the system, except those in Alaska and Hawaii, it is assumed, will be electronically interconnected by means of some 38,000 miles of coaxial cable or microwave relays. About 10,000 miles of circuitry is required for an interstate system connecting one point in each of the forty-eight contiguous states of the union to the national system, and over 28,000 miles for intrastate systems in forty-seven of those states. Eventually the stations may be interconnected by means of a celestial satellite, or some other improved mode of distribution. But the model under consideration assumed only the conventional means of interconnection by coaxial cable or microwave.

This system will be capable of carrying not only the thirty hours of programming for national distribution produced weekly under the auspices of the Corporation for Public Television, but also a substantial volume of programming to be distributed from producing stations to other stations wishing to broadcast it.

Each of the 210 originating stations is assumed to be equipped with two or more videotape units, at least one of them capable of handling programs in color. Each station can therefore, if it chooses, record incoming programs for subsequent broadcast, or, when the occasion warrants, broadcast a program simultaneously with its receipt, possibly within milliseconds of its creation.

The interstate system is assumed to be leased from the telephone system, the intrastate systems to be owned by the states or by organizations within the educational television system.

COSTS OF THE SYSTEM IN THE LONG RUN

Long Run Operating and Capital Costs

The annual operating costs of this system in the long run, as shown in Table 3, are estimated at $213 million and annual capital costs at $57 million, so that total costs are expected to be $270 million a year. About 80 percent of these costs, or $215 million a year, are those of the 380 stations, including $31 million annual costs of national programs produced by the key stations. Net of this item, the annual costs of the stations come to $184 million, or about 68 percent of the costs of the system. The remaining costs, besides the $31 million for national programs from key stations, are $23 million annually for national programs from producers other than stations, $17 million for national and state interconnection, and $15 million for the nonbroadcast activities of the Corporation for Public Television.

All these costs are estimated at prices and salary levels prevailing in 1967. To the extent that future prices and salary levels change, the estimates would have to be adjusted accordingly.

In the long run, the system will require capital investment of about $621 million, over 90 percent of it to be invested in the stations. Outside the stations about $50 million of capital is required, not counting the capital invested by parties external to the educational television system, principally the telephone system, and to a much lesser extent, the owners of studio facilities rented by independent producers. Of that $50 million, $42 million is the estimated capital costs of the intrastate connections, and $8 million the costs of the facilities at the two production centers, at $4 million each. That amount could pay for two fully equipped color studios at each center, each studio capable of supporting the production of two hours of programming per week or eight hours in all. The remaining two hours of national contract programming per week can be assumed to come from film production on location or possibly from programs produced elsewhere than at the facilities of the two centers.

TABLE 3

COSTS OF A FULLY DEVELOPED EDUCATIONAL
TELEVISION SYSTEM IN THE LONG RUN

Cost of:	Number or Amount	Capital Required	Annual Costs		
			Operating	Capital	Total
		(millions of dollars)			
Stations					
Key	20	124	60	12	72
Flag	40	132	47	11	58
Standard	75	127	37	12	49
Basic	75	95	12	10	22
Repeater	170	93	6	8	14
TOTAL	380	571	162	53	215
National Programs (excluding Key Station Production)	520 hrs/yr	8	23	b	23
Interconnection					
Interstate [a]	9,900 miles	—	9	—	9
Intrastate	28,000 miles	42	4	4	8
TOTAL			13	4	17
Corporation for Public Television (nonbroadcast activities)	—	—	15	—	15
TOTAL COSTS		621	213	57	270

[a] Interstate interconnections are assumed to be leased from the telephone system, so their capital costs are not included in these estimates. On the alternative assumption that the educational television system is to own its own interstate interconnection system, the capital cost of the interstate interconnection would be $30 million, and the annual costs about $6 million, $3 million for operating and $3 million for capital amortization. The leased cost is based on 8 hours of interconnection service daily, the owned system's costs could give 24 hours a day service, if desired.

[b] Carried in cost of programs.

References: *Stations:* Tables 17 and 18
National Programs: Table 20
Interconnection: Tables 18 and 19
Corporation for Public Television (nonbroadcast activities): Estimated by Commission staff

Costs of Functions Performed

The $270 million annual costs of the system are arranged in Table 4 so as to show the costs of the various functions performed by the system. It costs $50 million a year to deliver the educational television signal throughout the country, $54 million a year to produce an inflow of thirty hours a week of new national programs, and $151 million a year to enable the 210 originating stations to carry on their local origination. In this connection, origination means not only the production of local and exchange programs, the principal object of local origination costs, but also the costs associated with the ownership and operation of video-tape units and telecine equipment which permits the broadcast, at times selected by the station management, of programs produced elsewhere. It includes origination of instructional television programs, and local autonomy in their scheduling.

The $50 million cost of signal delivery is made up of $33 million for transmission, the annual operating and capital costs of the 380 transmitters, and $17 million for interconnection, both interstate and intrastate. The $54 million cost of national program production includes the $23 million worth of contract programming per year plus the $31 million cost of the 1040 hours per year of national programming produced in the key stations.

The cost of local origination is estimated by subtracting from the $215 million costs of station operation (Table 3) the costs, included in that total, of transmission ($33 million) and costs of national program production at key stations ($31 million). The remainder, $151 million, is the annual cost of achieving the Commission's goal of widespread local program production and of local control of the program schedule for both Public and instructional television.

About one half of the $621 million worth of capital required by the system is devoted to supporting local origination, about 40 percent supports signal delivery, and the remainder, a little more than 10 percent, supports the production of national programs.

TABLE 4

LONG–RUN COSTS OF FUNCTIONS PERFORMED BY A FULLY DEVELOPED EDUCATIONAL TELEVISION SYSTEM

	Number or Amount	Capital Required	Annual Costs		
			Operating	Capital	Total
	(millions of dollars)				
Signal Delivery					
Transmission Interconnection	380 stations	201	16	17	33
Interstate [a]	9,900 miles	—	9	—	9
Intrastate	28,000 miles	42	4	4	8
TOTAL		243	29	21	50
National Program Production					
By Stations	1,040 hrs/yr	60	29	2 [c]	31
By Others	520 hrs/yr	8 [b]	23	[c]	23
TOTAL		68	52	2	54
Local Origination	210 stations	310 [d]	117	34	151
Corporation for Public Television (nonbroadcast activities)		—	15	—	15
TOTAL COSTS		621	213	57	270

[a] See note *a* to Table 3.

[b] Excludes private capital in rented studios.

[c] Carried by cost of programs.

[d] Excluding $60 million of facilities furnished by the Corporation for Public Television to support key station national programming. These facilities also contribute to local and exchange programming; $4 million of the $6 million annual capital cost of these facilities charged to local origination, $2 million to national.

References: Transmitter Costs: Table 14; Interconnection: Tables 15 and 16; Local Origination: See text; National Program Production: Tables 20, 21; Corporation for Public Television: Estimated by Commission staff

The $60 million capital cost allocated to national pro-
gram production represents capital at the key stations to be
supported by the Corporation for Public Television in order
to permit them to have the facilities appropriate to the
production of national programs. Those facilities can, however, also be used for the production of local and exchange
programs for both Public and instructional television. Indeed, one of the principal reasons for the Commission's
recommendation that stations in as many as twenty localities
in the United States be assisted in acquiring the capability
of producing national programs is that the enhancement
of their skills and facilities will elevate the quality of their
local and exchange programs. Here, as at many other
points in the system, multiple objectives are served by the
arrangements, so that the allocation of a charge to a particular function does not do justice to the complexity of the
underlying interrelationships.

Costs of the Objectives

Table 5 affords yet another way of looking at the $270
million annual costs of the educational television system
in the long run. A bill is there drawn up for the whole
system, charging each objective with its estimated cost.
The first two items, signal delivery and national programming, have already been considered, with their costs placed
at $50 million and $54 million a year respectively.

Item 3, at $82 million, is the cost of providing scheduling
autonomy and about ten hours a week of locally originated
programming of the quality produced by flag stations for
each of forty-seven states and thirteen "substates," as we
may call the cultural areas of the secondary metropolises.
The cost of this objective is reckoned as the difference between the total costs of the 60 flag stations and their transmission costs, since this reflects the difference between
about ten hours of "flag station quality" local production
and programming autonomy on the one hand, and passive
program transmission on the other.

Item 4, costing $11 million, is the extra cost of local and
regional programming produced at the key stations above

TABLE 5

ITEMIZED ANNUAL BILL FOR EDUCATIONAL TELEVISION IN THE LONG RUN

Item No.	Objective	No. of Units	Per Unit	Subtotal	Total
			(millions of dollars)		
1.	Signal Delivery	*380 stations*			50
	a. Transmission to 94% of the Nation	337 stations	0.086	29	
	b. Second Service to ⅓ of the Nation	43 stations	0.083	4	
	c. Interconnection, National and State	38,000 miles		17	
2.	National Programming	*30 hrs./wk.*			54
	a. Contract programming	10 hrs./wk.	2.3	23	
	b. Key Stations	20 hrs./wk.	1.56	31	
3.	Programming Autonomy and 10 Hours of "Flag Style" Local Origination per Week	*60 stations*			82
	a. States	47 states	1.37	64.4	
	b. "Substates"	13 substates	1.37	17.8	
4.	10 Hours of "Key Style" Local Origination per Week	20 regions	0.57	11.4	11
5.	Programming Autonomy and 5 Hours of "Standard Style" Local Origination per Week	*75 stations*			42
	a. States	3 states	0.56	1.7	
	b. Medium-sized Metropolitan Areas	57 areas	0.56	31.9	
	c. State Capitals	15 capitals	0.56	8.4	

Annual Cost

	75 stations			
6. Programming Autonomy and 1 to 1½ Hours of "Basic Style" Local Origination Per Week				15
a. Small Metropolitan Areas	66 areas	0.2	13.2	
b. Very Small Metropolitan Areas	9 areas	0.2	1.8	
7. Health and Progress of Public Television through Nonbroadcast Activities of Corporation for Public Television				15
TOTAL				270 [a]

[a] Total differs from sum of column because of rounding.

Bases of Cost per Unit

1a Total annual costs per transmitter: average of 337 "first" stations, $86,000

1b Total annual costs per transmitter: costs of UHF transmitter for each of 43 "second" stations, $83,000

2a Annual cost of one hour per week of contract programming: 52 hours per year at $45,000 an hour, $2,340,000

2b Annual cost of one hour per week of key station national programming: 52 hours per year at $30,000 an hour, $1,560,000

3a,b Annual cost of local origination at a representative flag station: total annual costs less those of the transmitter, $1,370,000

4 Annual cost of 10 hours a week of "key style" local and regional programming in excess of cost of 10 hours a week of "flag style" programming: excess of $2.03 million annual cost of key station, net of national program costs, over $1.46 million total annual costs of flag station, $570,000

5a,b,c Annual cost of local origination at a representative standard station: total annual costs, less those of the transmitter, $560,000

6a,b Annual cost of local origination at a representative basic station: total annual costs, less those of the transmitter, $200,000 the cost of a comparable volume of programming produced at regular flag stations. It represents therefore, at least to a certain extent, the cost of a quality difference, the cost of having in each of twenty areas into which the country can be divided a source of local and regional programming fully equipped for color and capable of unusually high quality program production. In part, however, the $11 million also reflects the higher level of costs in the large metropolitan centers in which the key stations are located as compared with costs in the somewhat smaller metropolitan centers in which the regular flag stations are located.

Item 5, at $42 million, is the cost of providing "standard station style" local programming and schedule autonomy to the seventy-five areas projected to have standard stations, and Item 6, at $15 million, is the comparable figure for the basic stations. Item 7 is the cost, estimated also at $15 million, of the nonbroadcast activities of the Corporation, already noted in Tables 3 and 4.

Expenses of the Corporation in the Long Run

The principal activity of the Corporation for Public Television will be to arrange for the production, by the key stations and by the production centers or other program-contracting agencies, of thirty hours a week of national programming. In addition, it will work with the stations to aid and encourage their production of high quality local and exchange programs. To that end it will provide contributions to the stations in aid of local and exchange programming. It will also supply capital funds for those facilities of key stations and the production centers required for the production of national programs, or to elevate the standards of local and exchange programming.

It will be a continuing responsibility of the Corporation to support the interstate interconnection of the system. The Corporation is also charged with the responsibility for making grants in support of training programs for the technical, artistic, and other specialized personnel required by the educational television system, and for conducting

TABLE 6

CORPORATION FOR PUBLIC TELEVISION
Long-Run Costs

	Number or Amount	Annual Cost per Unit (thousands of dollars)	Total Costs (millions of dollars)
National Programs			
Produced by Key Stations	1,040 hrs/yr	30	31
Produced by Contractors	520 hrs/yr	45	23
Total			54
Interstate Interconnections	9,900 miles	0.870	9
Contributions in Aid of Local Programming			
To: Key Stations	20 stations	250	5.0
Regular Flag Stations	40 stations	200	8.0
Standard Stations	75 stations	100	7.5
Basic Stations	75 stations	25	1.8
Total			22
Capital Support to Key Stations	20 stations	200	4
Nonbroadcast Activities			15
Total			104

Sources: National Programs: Commission staff
Interstate Interconnections: Table 15
Contributions in Aid of Local Programming and Capital Support to Key Stations: Economic consultant to the Commission within guidelines set by Commission and staff
Nonbroadcast Activities: Commission staff

research. It will maintain a library of programs and will distribute these older programs as well as newly created programs to the educational television system. Furthermore, it will keep archives and in general engage in those activities likely to advance the art of Public Television or otherwise aid in its development.

The annual rate of expenses of the Corporation for Public Television for all purposes may be estimated at $104 million in the long run. As shown in Table 6, the principal object of these expenditures is the $54 million annual cost of production of national programs. Of this total, $31 million goes for the twenty hours per week of national programming produced by the key stations, and $23 million for ten hours per week of contract programs, produced principally at the two production centers. The average cost per hour of these programs is judged to be $30,000 and $45,000 respectively (Tables 20 and 21).

The $9 million annual costs of interstate interconnection will presumably be borne by the Corporation until some other arrangement is made. Eventually some of this burden may be lifted from the Corporation either by a rate reduction or by an arrangement permitting free use of communications satellite service.

The $22 million expense item for contributions in aid of local programming has not appeared in the previous tabulations of the costs of the system because it is a transfer payment from the Corporation to the stations. It represents that part of the local stations' costs of local and exchange program production that is borne by the Corporation. Exactly how the Corporation will go about making these contributions will ultimately be decided by the Corporation itself. For the purposes of estimation, however, we may think of the Corporation supporting worthwhile local programs at the rate of $2000 per hour. Alternatively, the Corporation might contribute a smaller fraction of the cost of a greater volume of programming, at a rate, say, of $500 per hour. In either case the Corporation could do much to support local programming both by the financial aid given and by the incentive offered by the potential availability of that aid. The estimates in Table 6 of the average contribution received per station claim to be no more than reasonable judgments of how the Corporation might find it best to distribute its contributions.

In addition, the Corporation will presumably support about $6 million a year of the annual capital costs of the key stations. This amount, half the annual capital costs of the key stations, represents the excess of the capital costs of a key station over those of a flag station. The difference is associated with the extra facilities required for the quality of programming, both national and local, which it is the responsibility of the Corporation to encourage at these stations. As shown in Table 2, the annual capital costs of a key station run about $300,000 a year higher than those of a flag station, so that for the 20 key stations the difference is $6 million. About $2 million of the $6 million will be indirectly charged to the Corporation in the depreciation costs included in the $31 million annual costs of the national programs produced by the key stations. The remaining $4 million of capital support from the Corporation to the key stations will presumably be made, in the long run, as a direct capital contribution as shown in Table 6.

The Corporation's annual expenses in the long run for nonbroadcast activities, outlined in Chapter 3 of the Commission's Report, have been estimated at $15 million.

Cost of Instructional Programs

The cost estimates of Table 3 were made without explicit reference to the production of instructional programs. The *broadcasting* of instructional programs has been provided for, and forty-five hours a week of the station's broadcast time is assumed to be devoted to that activity, and the corresponding costs are included in the totals of Table 3. But in conceptually staffing and running the stations and pricing out the cost of operations the assumptions about program production were appropriate to Public rather than to instructional television.

There are three possible ways of reconciling these cost estimates with alternative future states of instructional programming. The simplest is to regard that which has been priced out as a system for broadcasting both Public and instructional programming, but for producing only Public Television programs. The instructional programs can be conceived of as brought to the system on film or tape, as many are now in fact brought. The cost of their production must then be met elsewhere.

A second way of viewing the problem is to consider that only one shift per day has been counted on for studio use for Public programs. This leaves room for another daily shift for instructional program production. If such additional program production were actually undertaken, the costs of manning the extra shift would be additional to those included in Table 3.

A third way of viewing the matter is to regard the assumed pattern of use of the stations as only one of many possible patterns within the given cost structure. Without altering the total costs it would be possible to use some of the studio time and some of the production teams on instructional programming by cutting back on the production of Public programming.

In short, within these cost estimates there is room for a variety of accommodations to the future requirements of instructional programming. If those requirements are moderate they may even fit interstitially into the cost pattern of Public programming. If they are substantial, they may considerably reduce the volume of Public programming produced, or they may lead to costs additional to those entered into the estimates.

The reason the costs of instructional programming must be left in this indefinite state is that instructional television has not been given the study that would be necessary to make assumptions specific enough to price it out. What has been priced out is a system that can handle the needs of Public Television and can go a long way toward meeting the needs of instructional television, whatever they may be. The system's exact relationship to the needs of instructional television can certainly not be ascertained, however, until those needs are more clearly defined.

THE PROJECTED TIME PATTERN OF COSTS AND FINANCING

The General Time Pattern of Costs

During the early, formative years of the proposed educational television system, a pattern of expenditures will be required substantially different from that of the long run. In the beginning, larger capital expenditures will be needed to build up facilities, and much smaller operating expenses will be required than will be needed later when the system is fully developed. As projected in Table 7, the annual operating costs of the system might, if the financing is available, rise sharply from the current level of $40 mil-

TABLE 7

EDUCATIONAL TELEVISION SYSTEM
Operating and Capital Costs: 1966–71 and Long Run

	1966	1968	Average 1968–71	1971	1972–80	Long Run Steady State
			(millions of dollars annually)			
Operating Costs						
Stations (gross)[a]	32	54	83	109	136	162
Intrastate Interconnection	2	2	3	4	4	4
National Programs (contract)	4[b]	7	12	18	21	23
Interstate Interconnection	1[c]	4	7	9	9	9
Corporation for Public Television (non-broadcast activities)	1[d]	3	7	10	13	15
Total Operating	40	70	112	150	183	213
Capital Costs (annual)						
Stations	23	60	60	60	60	53
Intrastate Interconnections		4	4	4	4	4
National Production Center[e]	—	2	2	2	0	—
Total Capital Costs	23	66	66	66	64	57
Total Operating and Capital Costs (annual)	63	136	178	216	247	270

[a] See Table 9 for gross operating costs of stations, which include the costs of producing national programs at key stations.

[b] NET's purchase of contract programs other than from stations.

[c] NET's costs of distribution by tape.

[d] NET'S nonbroadcast expenses, 1966.

[e] Excluding depreciation charged to National Programs.

lion to $70 million in the first year of operation of the proposed new program, taken for definiteness to be the year 1968. They would continue to increase rapidly for the first four years of the program, to about $150 million in 1971, and thereafter more gradually to the long run level of $213 million, assumed, for convenience, to be reached in 1980.

Capital expenditures, on the other hand, are projected to run fairly steadily at a level of about $64 million a year over that period, taken as the 13 years from 1968 to 1980, during which the system is to be built up. They are put at $66 million in each of the first four years of the program to allow an extra $2 million a year for the construction, at the outset, of two national production centers, at $4 million each. Thereafter, annual capital costs are put at a steady $64 million a year until the system is fully built in 1980. In the long run, of course, capital expenditures will be necessary only to replace equipment and plant as it is retired, which is projected to require $57 million a year.

The Time Pattern of Financing

A possible pattern of financing of the projected expenditures is shown in Table 8. It is based on the assumption that the Corporation for Public Television will be able to finance $40 million of operating and capital expenditures in 1968, $76 million in 1971, and $104 million in 1980 and thereafter. It is further assumed that the Department of Health, Education, and Welfare (HEW) will ultimately come to finance half of the operating costs of the system not financed by the Corporation, gradually working up to that fraction by financing the principal share of the annual increments of operating costs. But it is assumed that the HEW contribution will be offered in such a way as always to be associated with increased contributions from others, rather than permitting others to reduce their contributions.

As far as capital expenditures are concerned, the Corporation will, in the first four years, support to the extent of $2 million a year the construction of two national production centers. No capital costs of these centers are charged explicitly to the system thereafter since the depreciation on the centers will, it is presumed, be charged into the costs of the programs produced at the centers, and so will be implicitly included in the system's operating costs.

The Corporation will also, in the first seven or eight

TABLE 8

EDUCATIONAL TELEVISION SYSTEM
Possible Pattern of Financing: 1966–71 and Long Run

	1966	1968	Average 1968–71	1971	Average 1972–80	Long Run
			(millions of dollars)			
Operating Costs	40	70	112	150	183	213
Financed by:						
Corporation						
National Programs	5[a]	10	20[b]	31[b]	43[b]	52[b]
Local Programs	—	10	11	15	19	22
Interstate Interconnection	1[a]	5	7	9	9	9
Nonbroadcast Activities	1[a]	3	7	10	12	15
Total	7[a]	28	45	65	83	98
HEW and Others	33	42	67	85	100	115
HEW	—	6	31	42	50	57
Others	33	36	36	43	50	58
Capital Costs (annual)	23	66	66	66	64	57
Financed by:						
Corporation						
In Programs	—	—	1	1	2	2
Directly	—	12	10	10	5	4
Total	—	12	11	11	7	6
HEW and Others	23	54	55	55	57	51
HEW	7	36	37	37	38	34
Others	16	18	18	18	19	17
Total Costs, Operating and Capital	63	136	178	216	247	270
Financed by:						
Corporation	7[a]	40	56	76	90	104
HEW	7	42	68	79	88	91
Others	49	54	54	61	69	75

[a] 1966 data apply to NET, regarded as predecessor corporation.

[b] 7.3% of the cost of national programs from key stations represents depreciation and is deducted from this figure.

Operating Costs Financed by HEW: In the long run, 50% of operating costs not borne by Corporation, based on dollar-for-dollar matching ratio. In early years projected on assumption that HEW will structure incentives so that it will bear only incremental operating expenses, but a major share of those

Capital Costs Financed by HEW: Based on matching ratio of $2 from HEW to $1 from others, exclusive of the Corporation for Public Television

Sources: Operating and Capital Costs: Table 7
Expenditures of Corporation: Table 13

years of the program, finance at a rate assumed to average about $8 million a year, the $60 million worth of capital assets that the key stations require over and above those they would have if they simply remained flag stations. After the full $60 million of these capital assets has been financed, the corporation, as previously noted, is to continue to make a direct capital contribution of $4 million a year to the key stations toward the $6 million annual costs of amortization of the $60 million worth of capital assets. The remaining $2 million of the $6 million annual capital amortization also comes from the Corporation, but indirectly, as the depreciation component of the $31 million a year paid to the key stations by the Corporation in return for the national programming produced by those stations.

Capital costs other than those borne by the Corporation are to be financed, it is assumed, by HEW and "Others" on a matching basis of two dollars from HEW for every dollar available from "Others" for capital expenditures. "Others" includes, of course, state and local governments, foundations and other private sources, and the general public. The three-way sharing of aggregate costs among the Corporation, HEW, and "Others" is estimated to run at 29 percent, 31 percent, and 40 percent respectively in 1968 and gradually to switch to 38 percent, 34 percent, and 28 percent in the long run, as a consequence of the changing composition of total costs. If the assumed matching ratios are used, the funds coming from "Others" will have to be raised to $75 million by 1980, if the system is to achieve full scale operation at that time. No estimate has been made as to whether or not this amount will actually be forthcoming, merely that it will be required under the assumed matching ratios.

Operating Costs

Stations. As sketched out in Table 12, it is estimated that the assumed $60 million annual rate of capital expenditures for station facilities in the buildup period will support the establishment of 90 new stations in the three years from January 1, 1968, to January 1, 1971, distributed among

TABLE 9

NUMBER OF STATIONS AND STATION OPERATING COSTS[a], 1966–80

(Reported for 1966, Projected, 1968–80)

	Full Scale Net Operating Costs per station[a]	1966		1968		1971		1980	
		Number of Stations[b]	Full-Scale Costs	Number of Stations[b]	Full-Scale Costs	Number of Stations[b]	Full-Scale Costs	Number of Stations[b]	Full-Scale Costs
	(thousands of dollars)		(millions of dollars)		(millions of dollars)		(millions of dollars)		(millions of dollars)
Key	1,550	20	31	20	31	20	31	20	31
Flag	1,180	24	28	35	41	40	47	40	47
Standard	490	40	20	50	25	75	37	75	37
Basic	156	15	2	25	4	75	12	75	12
Repeater	38	14	1	20	1	30	1	170	6
Total		113	82	150	102	240	128	380	133
Percent of Scale		37%		50%		75%		100%	
Operating Costs (net)		31c		51		96		133	
Cost of National Programs Produced at Key Stations[d]			1		3		13		29
Operating Costs (gross)			32		54		109		162

a Excludes depreciation, and for each key station also excludes $1,560,000 (less 7.3% for depreciation) charged to Corporation for Public Television for production of programs for national distribution.

b Number on the air over the year.

c Roughly estimated from reported figure of $34.3 by deducting $1.6 million as charged to NET for national programs, and $2 million for intrastate interconnections.

d Excluding 7.3% allowance for depreciation.

References: Full-Scale Station Costs: Table 17; Number of Stations: Table 12

ultimate station types as shown in that table. There are
124 educational stations on the air now, at the beginning
of 1967. By January 1, 1968, there will probably be 150,
so that by January 1, 1971, under the program here projected, there would be 240 stations on the air, including all
210 stations projected to be eventually capable of program
origination. If each of these stations were to incur the full-
scale level of operating expenses given in Table 2, and
detailed in Table 17, the 1971 net operating costs would
be $128 million, as shown in Table 9.[5] These full-scale ex-
penses of any station refer to the expenses of the station
that it is someday to become, not the station that it actually
is in the year under consideration. The $31 million net
operating expenses of stations on the air in 1966, as shown
in Table 9, for example, came to about 37 percent of the
level of net costs that would have been incurred if those
stations had operated at their long-run full scale, the representative cost levels given in Tables 2 and 17.

It seems reasonable therefore to project a gradual
growth of the breadth and intensity of each station's activities as the program develops. At the initiation of the
program in 1968, however, the level of operations might
be raised from the current 37 percent to 50 percent of full
scale, with 75 percent of scale achieved by 1971 and 100
percent only in the long run, taken as the year 1980. It
is on this assumption that the projected net operating costs
of Table 9 were derived. To convert them to the gross
operating costs given in the first line of Table 7, it is necessary to project the costs of the national programming likely
to be produced by the key stations each year from 1968 to
1971. For the long run, this figure has already been projected (Table 4) at $31 million, of which the operating
cost component is $29 million.

It cannot be expected that national programming, de-

[5] In this connection, "net" operating costs of the stations are the
total operating costs minus the operating cost component (92.7 percent) of costs of the key stations for production of national programs.
"Gross" operating costs of the stations are the station's operating costs
before any deductions for the costs of national programs.

manding as it does creative skill of the highest order, can approach long-run full scale as rapidly as can the local programming of the stations. The operating costs of production of national programs at key stations are therefore projected, in Table 9, at $3 million in 1968, at $13 million in 1971, and only gradually thereafter will the operating costs of national programming produced in key stations approach the long-run level of $29 million a year.

Other Operating Costs. The production of national contract programs, the largest remaining element in operating costs of the system, is not subject to the same constraints on its rate of growth as is the production of national programs by the key stations. The total amount of contract programming to be demanded by Public Television is not likely to press hard on the resources available to the television industry, upon which Public Television can draw. The rate of growth of expenditures on contract programs must accordingly be governed by considerations of how much it is worthwhile to spend on them within the available budget of the Corporation, given its other objectives. It seems reasonable to project in Table 7 a rapid increase of expenditures other than with stations from the $4 million level of 1966 to $7 million in 1968 and to $18 million in 1971. The rate of increase thereafter is projected to be much slower, as increases in expenditures on national programming are channeled more and more to the key stations, whose capabilities will have been steadily developing.

The annual operating costs of intrastate interconnections were projected to approach rapidly their long-run level of $4 million. This judgment was based on the consideration that the early operating expenditures for intrastate interconnection would be largely for leased lines, fairly rapidly available, and more expensive per mile on an annual basis than owned microwave facilities. Gradually, a shift would be made to owned facilities, so the increase in the number of stations served would, roughly, be counterbalanced by the reduction in average cost per mile. A level figure of $4 million a year accordingly seemed appropriate from 1971 on.

The annual cost of interstate interconnection was also projected as rising rapidly to its long-run level of $9 million, but for different reasons. To serve the forty-eight contiguous states will cost the same amount irrespective of the number of stations within each state. And the leasing rate structure is such that there are no substantial economies from using less than eight hours a day. So the interstate interconnection cost was assumed to reach its full level of $9 million by about 1970.

Finally, the nonbroadcast expenditures of the Corporation for Public Television were assumed to achieve two-thirds of their long-run level by 1971, the fourth year of its operation.

The Time Pattern of Capital Costs

Stations. An estimated annual capital cost of $60 million for the stations during the buildup period of the educational television system was adopted as the most reasonable compromise between a substantially higher figure that would yield an earlier attainment of a fully developed system and moderately lower figures that would unduly postpone that attainment.

In the long run, there is to be $571 million invested in the stations (Table 10). If this were to be achieved in seven years, an investment rate of a little less than $80 million a year would suffice, since that would account for $560 million, and more than $11 million of capital assets would remain from those in use at the beginning of the seven-year period. But any rate of investment that takes more than seven years to build the system up to full scale must take account of the fact that studio equipment usually has a life of no more than seven years, transmitter equipment no more than ten. Equipment put in place early in any period of duration greater than seven or ten years will therefore be retired before the end of that period. Consequently, the most rapid way to build up the system with an investment rate of less than $80 million a year would be to concentrate on land and plant first and equipment later. An investment rate of $60 million a year could,

TABLE 10

CAPITAL ASSETS OF EDUCATIONAL TELEVISION STATIONS IN THE LONG RUN

Type of Station	No. of Stations	Land		Structures		Equipment at Studio and Mobile		Equipment at Transmitter		All Capital
		Value per Station (thousands of dollars)	Total Value (millions of dollars)	Value per Station (thousands of dollars)	Total Value (millions of dollars)	Value per Station (thousands of dollars)	Total Value (millions of dollars)	Value per Station[a] (thousands of dollars)	Total Value (millions of dollars)	Total Value (millions of dollars)
Key	40	578	11.6	1,675	33.5	3,608	72.2	359	7.2	124.5
Flag	40	208	8.3	1,232	49.2	1,473	58.8	381	15.2	131.5
Standard	75	70	5.2	487	36.5	730	54.7	403	30.2	126.6
Basic	75	26	2.0	252	18.9	575	43.1	409	31.3	95.3
Repeater	170	1	0.2	117	19.9	—	—	431	73.2	93.3
Total			27.3		158.0		228.8		157.1	571.2
Years of Life		∞		30		7		10		—
Annual Capital Cost, Long Run			—		5.2		32.0[b]		15.7	52.9

[a] Weighted average of 309 for VHF, 453 for UHF, weighted according to frequency within station type group.
[b] Excluding $0.7 million for videotape replacement, expensed annually.

Source: Industrial and economic consultants to the Commission

for example, achieve a fully developed system in less than nine and a half years if there were to be no concern for balance among the various components of investment in the early years: by first investing in land and plant and transmitter equipment, and then in studio equipment. But actually it is much more sensible, and more in accord with the needs of the program, to undertake a balanced rate of investment at the cost of taking a few more years to achieve a fully developed system. Nonetheless, it seemed best to move a little way from strict balance by conceptually adopting a two-phase program giving somewhat greater than proportional emphasis to bricks and mortar in the first phase of six years, and to studio and mobile equipment in the second phase of seven years. Such a scheme is illustrated in Table 11.

TABLE 11

EDUCATIONAL TELEVISION STATIONS
Two-Phase 13-Year Capital Investment Program

	Total Capital Required in Steady State (1)	Amount Available at End of Period from Initial Stock (2)	Annual Investment		Amount Available at End of Period (5)
			First Phase (6 years) (3)	Second Phase (7 years) (4)	
	(millions of dollars)				
Buildings and Land	185	10	15.6	11.6	185
Equipment, Studio and Mobile	229	—	15.7	32.7	229
Equipment, Transmitter	157	—	28.7	15.7	157
TOTAL	571	10	60	60	571

Sources: Col. 1, Table 10
Col. 2, Rough estimate of land and buildings surviving out of initial stock; see text
Cols. 3 and 4, Projected by economic consultant to the Commission to meet requirements
Col. 5, Col. 2 plus cumulated investment for X years for each type of asset, where X equals the number of years of life of that asset (Table 10) or 13 years, whichever is smaller

A reasonable pattern of distribution among the stations of the $180 million investment in station facilities assumed for the first three years of the program is shown in Table 12. The number of stations in existence at the beginning of 1968, classified by type of station to which their community would entitle them by the criteria adopted (Table 1) was estimated from the distribution of the characteristics of metropolitan areas with stations on the air in 1966 together with those which had construction permits for new stations. It was assumed that a construction permit for a station in a large metropolitan area has a higher probability of being soon converted to a license for an operating station than does one for a smaller community.

The aggregate long-run capital requirements of the existing stations estimated as of January 1, 1968, comes to $367 million (Table 12). That is what their total capital would amount to if each station on the air in 1968 were actually to have an amount of capital equal to the average long-run figure for the capital of a station in a community of its type as given in Tables 2 and 18. The original value of the capital likely to be actually in place at these stations as of January 1, 1968, is probably of the order of only $70 million to $80 million, since the accumulated investment up to 1966 was about $85 million, with perhaps another $23 million to come in 1967, and by that time accumulated retirements could well be between $26 million and $36 million.

If, as projected in Table 12, these "existing" stations are to put in place new capital assets to the amount of $112 million in the three years 1968–1970, they would have by January 1971 about $160 million to $170 million of capital in place, after allowing for about $20 million of retirements over the three years. They would accordingly be equipped in 1971 at about 45 percent of the full-scale level of $367 million for these stations. Meanwhile, the new stations with $68 million of brand-new capital projected to be in place by 1971 would by that year have a ratio of capital in place to long-run capital requirements of over 50 percent. This difference is, however, justified by

TABLE 12

PROJECTED CAPITAL EXPENDITURE PATTERN FOR STATIONS

First Three Years, 1968–70

	Key (A)	Key (B)[a]	Flag	Standard	Basic	Repeater	Total
FULL-SCALE CAPITAL PER STATION	6.2	6.2	3.3	1.7	1.3	0.55	
EXISTING STATIONS (1/1/68)							
Number	10	10	35	50	25	20	150
Investment per Station. 1968–70 (millions of dollars)	2.0	1.5	1.0	0.6	0.4	0.1	
Total for Period, 1968–70 (millions of dollars)	20	15	35	30	10	2	112
Long-Run Capital Required (millions of dollars)	62	62	115	85	32	11	367
NEW STATIONS ESTABLISHED (1968–70)							
Number	—	—	5	25	50	10	90
3-Year Investment per Station (millions of dollars)	—	—	1.6	1.0	0.6	0.5	
Total 3-Year Investment (millions of dollars)	—	—	8	25	30	5	68
Long-Run Capital Required (millions of dollars)	—	—	17	42	65	6	130
STATIONS IN EXISTENCE (1/1/71)							
Number	10	10	40	75	75	30	240
Total 3-Year Investment (millions of dollars)	20	15	43	55	40	7	180
Long-Run Capital Required (millions of dollars)	62	62	132	127	97	17	497

[a] A B-type key station is one which is ultimately to be a key station, but has not attained key status in this period.

References: Full-Scale Capital per Station: Table 18
Investment per Station: Projection by economic consultant within constraints set by data of Table 11

the fact that the new stations are more heavily concentrated in the standard and basic classifications, and in these classifications capital costs of transmitter and tower, while the same in dollars and cents as for the larger stations, are *relatively* greater than for larger stations. Since it would not make sense to build, at these new stations, smaller towers than they require in the long run, or to equip them with transmitters less than the full practical power planned for the long run, they would initially have about $500,000 each invested in transmitter, tower, and auxiliary equipment. The investment pattern of Table 11 works out so that in these early years of the program the new stations would be, on the average, better equipped for transmission, but much less completely equipped in studio and mobile equipment, than the older stations in comparable communities. In the later years of the program both new and old stations would be brought up to full scale with respect to both production and transmission facilities.

In any case, the $60 million annual rate of capital investment in stations could suffice, in the first three years of the program, to put on the air all the new stations required in the long run for program origination, and also to improve the equipment of the stations already on the air in 1968 from that year's level of less than one-fourth full scale to close to 50 percent of full scale at the end of 1971.

It would take another ten years, however, to complete the program shown in Table 11, bringing the facilities of the 210 program-originating stations up to long-run full scale, and bringing into service 140 repeater stations in addition to the thirty projected to be on the air by the end of 1971. During this period the operating activities of the stations can also steadily approach full scale as pictured in Table 9.

Other Capital Costs. The capital costs other than those of stations were projected as steady rates of investment over the assumed periods of completion. The intrastate microwave systems were estimated, Table 16, below, to require $42 million of capital investment. Once built they will presumably require 10 percent a year capital replace-

ment. It was accordingly assumed that capital expenditures
on these microwave systems would proceed at the rate of
$4.2 million a year, so as to build the system in ten years.
The systems would thereafter require $4.2 million a year
in replacement costs, at least until some new distribution
system, by satellite or otherwise, replaces them.

The $8 million worth of production center facilities are
projected as being completed in four years at a rate of $2
million a year. Their capital costs for replacement thereafter can be covered out of the allowances for capital amortization charged against the expenses of programs produced
at the centers.

TABLE 13

CORPORATION FOR PUBLIC TELEVISION

Projected Expenditures

	1968	Average 1968–71	1971	Average 1972–80	Long Run Steady State
		(millions of dollars)			
National Programs					
From Stations	3	9	14	24	31
From Contract	7	12	18	21	23
	10	21	32	45	54
Contributions in Aid of Local and Regional Program-ming	10	11	15	19	22
Interstate Inter-Connection	5	7	9	9	9
Nonbroadcast Activities	3	7	10	12	15
Capital Contributions					
Key Stations	10	8	8	5	4
Production Center	2	2	2	0	0
	12	10	10	5	4
Total Expenditures	40	56	76	90	104

Source: Projected by economic consultant within guidelines set by
Commission and staff

Expenditures of the Corporation for Public Television

The projected time pattern of the expenditures of the Corporation for Public Television, implicitly or explicitly included in the estimates so far given, are summarized in Table 13. The derivations of the estimates of all expenditures of the Corporation except the contributions in aid of local and regional programming have already been summarized. Those latter contributions have been projected to start at about $10 million in 1968, thus supporting over 60 percent of the $16 million increase in net operating expenses of the stations in 1968 required to raise their operating level from 37 percent of scale, which can be presumed to be characteristic of 1967 as it was of 1966, to the 50 percent of scale that is the target for 1968. The remaining $6 million is assumed to come from HEW.

The $10 million Corporation contribution works out to an average of $77,000 per originating station projected to be on the air in 1968, but it cannot be assumed to be equally distributed, since its allocation will be governed by the ability of the stations to produce, with the aid of the contributions, local and regional programming worthy of support. As time goes on, not only will there be more stations offering programs worthy of support, but each station will be able to produce more programs of this quality, so the average contribution received per station can be expected to increase. The long-run level of the contribution received per station is not expected to cover all the costs of programming related to program content, but a sufficiently large proportion of such costs as to make a major contribution to the support of local and regional programming.

BASES OF THE ESTIMATES

The costs of the broadcast activities of the educational television system under consideration are determined by five factors:

1. The number of stations in the system.
2. The costs of interconnection.
3. The number of stations of each type.

4. The costs of each type of station.

5. The costs of national programs.

The considerations governing the projected size of each factor will be examined in turn.

Number of Stations

The basic economics of television coverage can be summarized in the rough estimate that the incremental cost to the system of adding one more television transmitter at full practical power averages about $115,000 a year (Table 14). Of this, $85,000 a year goes for the annual operating and capital costs of the transmitter, and $30,000 for interconnection. The $85,000 annual costs of the transmitter

TABLE 14

INCREMENTAL ANNUAL COST TO THE SYSTEM OF ONE MORE TELEVISION TRANSMITTER

	VHF	UHF	Weighted[a] Average
	(thousands of dollars annually)		
OPERATING EXPENSES			
Engineering Attendance[b]	29	0[b]	4.4
Engineering Maintenance	10	10	10.0
Electricity	6	11	10.4
Replacement Parts	13	13	13
Total	58	34	38
CAPITAL AMORTIZATION			
Tower and Building	4	4	4
Equipment	31	45	43
Total	35	49	47
Total Transmission	93	83	85
INTERCONNECTION	30	30	30
Total	123	113	115

a Weights: VHF 26, UHF 144, relative frequencies among repeater stations.

b UHF transmitters may run unattended, VHF may not.

Source: Industrial consultants to the Commission

is a weighted average of $83,000 a year for an unattended UHF transmitter and $93,000 a year for a VHF transmitter, including, for the latter, $29,000 for engineering attendance.

The annual cost of $30,000 for interconnection of an additional station to an interstate microwave loop is based on a requirement per station of 100 miles of relay at an estimated cost of $300 a year per mile (Table 16). The average station's distance from the rest of the system is smaller, about 86 miles, but a station in a sparsely settled area on the margin of consideration is likely to be at greater than average distance from the rest of the system.

The estimated coverage of the system and the cost of that coverage then depend on the criteria adopted for a given city to have a station. The principal criterion used in this model was that a city is to have a station in the long run if that station extends educational television coverage to an area in which 70,000 people will be living in 1980,[6] and not receiving service from any other educational television station. A marginal station, costing $115,000 a year for operation, capital cost, and interconnection, thus implies an incremental cost per capita of $1.64.

This cutoff criterion, plus such other criteria as that each metropolitan area with 1980 population over 140,000 will have its own station if it does not receive a grade A signal from some larger city, and that each state capital will receive a grade A signal, implies the existence of about 337 stations in the entire system, covering 94 percent of the population.

The per capita cost of the entire system comes to about $1.15 a year, the quotient of the $270 million annual costs of the system (Table 3) by the estimated coverage of 235 million out of a total 1980 population of 250 million. It would hardly be sensible to place the cutoff coverage criterion for a repeater station any higher than a population of 100,000, for which the incremental cost per capita would

[6] The population coverage criterion actually used was 50,000 people according to the 1960 census, taken to be the equivalent of 70,000 by 1980, since the official projections of the U.S. population indicate about a 40 percent increase for the nation as a whole between 1960 and 1980.

be $1.15, equal to the per capita cost of the system as a whole. By a well known proposition of economics, the average cost per capita of the system will be minimized by that cutoff criterion which sets the incremental cost per capita equal to the average cost per capita. It may, however, very well be deemed worthwhile to extend the cutoff point to a smaller population than that which minimizes average cost per capita. In those activities, such as national advertising, where problems of this sort frequently arise, it is generally found worthwhile to extend coverage well beyond the point of minimum average cost. The basic question is how much it is worth per capita to extend educational television. The implicit answer embodied in this model is $1.64 per year.

If a different judgment were made, and the incremental value of extending educational television service to one more person was set, say, at $1.15 per year, and the corresponding cutoff point was put at 100,000 people on a 1980 basis, the number of stations required would be reduced by 15 for a saving of $1.7 million in annual operating and capital costs for the 15 transmitters and their interconnection with the intrastate microwave systems, at $115,-000 each. Elimination of these 15 stations would deny coverage to 1.3 million people in 1980. The coverage would accordingly be reduced by 0.5 percent at a saving of about 0.6 percent of the total annual cost of the system. The denial of service would extend to both Public and instructional television, since these transmitters would be used jointly for the two purposes.

On the other hand, the opportunity for increasing coverage by installing full powered stations to serve areas with 1980 populations smaller than 70,000 seems very limited. If, for example, the cutoff point were lowered to 56,000 on a 1980 basis, fewer than 10 additional stations would be required. It seems that the sparsely populated areas not reached by the 380 transmitters of the model can more efficiently be reached by smaller transmitters taking a signal off the air at an adjacent mountain top or elevated point and rebroadcasting it over a modest unattended repeater transmitter. The cost of small transmitters of this sort would not be a significant component of the total cost of the system. In addition, many of these hard to reach areas are already served by community antenna systems, and if educational services become available in neighboring areas they can be brought to these communities over their community antenna systems, along with the commercial television services.

On considerations such as these the model was constructed with a cutoff population of 70,000 on a 1980 basis. A simulated design of a nationwide system of stations meeting these criteria indicated that 337 stations were required for national coverage so defined.

An additional 43 "second" stations in the great metropolitan areas were justified by the consideration that they could bring a second service to over one-third of the country's population for about $3.6 million a year, the annual operating and capital costs of 43 UHF transmitters. A second station in any city does not require any interconnection costs other than the expense of a microwave channel from the station to the transmitter, to be added to the microwave link already existing for the "first" station. On the assumption that each of these 43 stations would be run as an auxiliary outlet of the first station in its area, its programming costs could largely be covered by those already attributed to the associated first station. The incremental annual cost of the second station in each city would therefore be little more than the $83,000 annual cost of a UHF transmitter.

The total number of stations included in the model was accordingly 380.

Interconnection Costs

The annual costs of $9 million for interstate interconnection are those required to distribute the video and audio signals over 9900 miles of circuitry, eight hours a day, to one point in each of the forty-eight contiguous states and the District of Columbia with appropriate switching and terminal arrangements.

TABLE 15

EDUCATIONAL TELEVISION SYSTEM
INTERSTATE INTERCONNECTION SYSTEM COSTS

	No. of Miles	Cost per Mile/yr.	Total Annual Cost
		(dollars)	(millions of dollars)
Long-Distance Channels			
Two-way Video (type 7001)	4,700	840	3.95
Two-way Audio (type 6005)	4,700	108	0.51
One-way Video (type 7001)	5,200	420	2.19
One-way Audio (type 6005)	5,200	54	0.28
Lines, Total	9,900	700	6.93
Connections			1.02
Local Channels			.38
Switching and Miscellaneous			.30
TOTAL	9,900	870a	8.60

a Average.

Source: Industrial consultants to the Commission

These costs were estimated by conceptually designing a 9900-mile circuit, part of it offering two-way communication and part one-way, so that there could be many points at which programs could regularly be originated and sent in either direction, and there would be flexibility, permitting breaking the communication network into independent regional components. With one-way lines, video and audio, of the quality required available at $474 a mile per year, and two-way at $948, the long distance channels averaged out at a cost of $700 a mile (Table 15). Charges for the various connection arrangements required by the system, for the provision of local channels from telephone exchanges to each state's receiving point, and for switching charges for temporary system modifications for special events originating at other than regular points of origin, add another $1.7 million, or an average of $170 a mile, to make the overall average cost about $870 a mile. The total cost of the interstate system was accordingly estimated at about $9 million a year.

If the interstate connections were to be owned and operated by the educational television system, instead of being leased from the telephone system, there would be, it is estimated, an annual saving of about $3 million in operating expenses, but an increased capital cost of about $30 million. Owned lines could, however, be used twenty-four hours a day while the leased lines, at the price entered here, would be available on an eight hour a day basis only. If the needs of the system should grow so as to require substantially more than eight hours of interstate interconnection a day, it would then become increasingly advantageous to own an interstate microwave system instead of leasing the service.

There is, of course, a newly emerging possibility of a radically changed technology of interconnection by means of a celestial satellite. It has been proposed that interconnection service, either by satellite or by terrestrial circuitry, be made available free to educational television, or at greatly reduced rates. It has also been proposed that profits from the use of satellites by commercial broadcasters or other potential users be devoted to the support of educational television. Neither the possibility of reduced charges for interconnection, nor of revenues from satellite profits, has been entered into these estimates.

The intrastate circuits of the system will almost certainly be used for both instructional and Public programs, and so they will be required for more nearly the full broadcast day. Furthermore, somewhat less stringent standards of performance can be tolerated in an intrastate system than in a national system. Obviously, more microwave hops are required to cover the country than to cover a single state, and each hop contributes a certain degradation of the signal, the extent of the deterioration depending on the quality of the circuitry used. Consequently, the reliability tolerances need not be so close in an intrastate system as in the national system, and a more economical mode of operation is accordingly possible for intrastate circuits.

It was therefore judged that the intrastate interconnections could more advantageously be owned than leased.

TABLE 16

INTRASTATE INTERCONNECTION COSTS

	Number of States	Number of Station Points	Average Miles per Station	Total Miles of Relays	Cost per Mile	Total Cost
					(dollars)	(millions of dollars)
CAPITAL COSTS						
East of Mississippi	25	183	65	11,895		
West of Mississippi	22	147	105	16,170		
Total	47a	330b	86	28,065	1,500	42
ANNUAL COSTS						
Annual Operating and Maintenance (@10%)				28,065	150	4.2
Annual Capital Amortization (@10%)				28,065	150	4.2
Total Annual Costs					300	8.4

a Rhode Island, Alaska and Hawaii are assumed to have no intrastate microwave systems.
b There are 43 station points that serve two stations; 7 stations are in the 3 states and the District of Columbia with-out microwave systems.

Microwave circuits of the quality appropriate for this service can be constructed, it was estimated, at a comprehensive cost of $1500 per mile. The annual costs of operation were estimated at $150 per mile, and the amortization of capital at ten years' life would cost another $150 per mile annually. The total costs of intrastate interconnection were thus estimated as $300 per mile per year. The average mileage of the link connecting each station to its microwave loop was estimated at 65 miles east of the Mississippi and 105 miles west of the Mississippi, averaging 86 miles per station for the country as a whole (Table 16). For the 330 station points in contiguous United States, counting cities that have two stations as a single station point, the total mileage of intrastate interconnection comes to 28,065. This mileage multiplied by the cost per mile previously given, implies an annual cost for intrastate connection of $8.4 million, divided equally between operating and capital costs.

Number of Stations of Each Type

The station cost estimates, for both capital and annual costs, as shown in Table 3, were obtained simply by multiplying the number of stations of each type, projected in Table 1, by the costs of a representative station of that type. The criteria of Table 1 therefore critically govern the estimated station costs of the model. Any modification of these estimated costs would therefore require a corresponding change in the characteristics, and hence the number, of the metropolitan areas associated with any particular representative type of station.

If, for example, the representative standard station should be typical of larger metropolitan areas than has been assumed — say, of areas with 1980 population ranging from 500,000 to 1 million instead of from 300,000 to 1 million — 35 fewer stations would be in the standard class and 35 more in the basic class, and the estimated total annual costs of the system would be about $13 million lower, at $257 million instead of $270 million. If, in addition, contrary to assumption, there were no tendency for

TABLE 17

OPERATING EXPENSES AND ANNUAL
CAPITAL COSTS OF REPRESENTATIVE STATIONS

	Key	Flag	Standard	Basic	Repeater
OPERATING EXPENSES			(thousands of dollars)		
Salaries					
Managerial	327	138	77	20	—
Engineering	308	216	105	51	—
Operating Crews	289	164	36	10	—
Television Program Creation	542	160	44	—	—
Film Production Unit	221	73	24	—	—
Scenic and Graphic	100	24	7	—	—
Secretarial and Clerical	90	60	20	5	—
Supplements	97	65	20	—	—
TOTAL	1,974	900	333	86	—
OTHER OPERATING EXPENSES					
Talent, Fees, and Program Materials	287	54	20		
Program Supplies	477	81	40	28	—
General Expenses	207	95	59		
TOTAL	971	230	119		
Transmitter Operation[a]	50	46	42	41	38
Total Operating Expense	2,995	1,176	494	155	38
CAPITAL AMORTIZATION					
(annual)					
Structures (30 years life)	56	41	17	9	4
Studio and Mobile Equipment (7 years life)	506	203	100	81	—
Transmitter Equipment (10 years life)[a]	36	38	40	41	43
TOTAL	598	282	157	131	47
Total Annual Costs	3,593	1,458	651	286	85

[a] Weighted average of UHF and VHF. Weights vary with type of station.
Source: Economic and industrial consultants to the Commission

TABLE 18

CAPITAL REQUIREMENTS OF
REPRESENTATIVE STATIONS

	Key	Flag	Standard	Basic	Repeater
			(thousands of dollars)		
BUILDINGS AND LAND					
Studio and Office	2,135	1,322	439	160	—
EQUIPMENT					
Studio					
Studio Equipment[a]	995	335	181	143	—
Terminal Equipment[b]	147	97	74	74	—
Film and Tape Units	741	425	268	268	—
Film Editing Equipment	43	25	16	—	—
Lighting	133	55	17	9	—
Installation	338	141	83	74	—
TOTAL	2,597	1,078	638	568	—
Field					
Mobile Unit	889	288	40	—	—
Film Equipment	12	12	12	—	—
TOTAL	901	300	52	—	—
Miscellaneous					
Office Furniture	60	43	14	2	—
Videotape Stock	50	50	25	5	—
TOTAL	110	93	39	7	—
TOTAL EQUIPMENT					
Studio and Mobile	3,608	1,473	730	575	—
TRANSMITTER					
Tower and Building	118	118	118	118	118
Transmitter[c]	359	381	403	409	431
TOTAL	477	499	521	527	549
Total Structures and Land	2,253	1,440	557	278	118
Total Equipment	3,967	1,854	1,133	982	431
Total Capital Required	6,220	3,294	1,690	1,262	549

[a] Including camera chains, audio, master control, switching systems, and auxiliary equipment.

[b] Synchronization generators, distribution amplifiers, and equipment for color transmission.

[c] Weighted average of 453 for UHF and 309 for VHF, weighted according to the proportions in each station type group.
Source: Industrial consultants to the Commission

TABLE 19

PERSONNEL REQUIREMENTS OF A REPRESENTATIVE ORIGINATING STATION ACCORDING TO ITS TYPE

Type of Station

	Key		Flag		Standard		Basic	
	Number	Total Salary (thousands of dollars)	Number	Total Salary (thousands of dollars)	Number	Total Salary (thousands of dollars)	Number	Total Salary (thousands of dollars)
Management								
General Manager and Legal Counsel	2	45	1	20				
Program Manager and Assistants	2	37	1	15	1	15		
Production Manager and Assistant	2	37	1	15				
Director of Engineering and Assistants	3	49	1	15	1	12		
Scheduling Director and Assistants	2	30	1	12	1	12	2	20
Business Manager and Assistants	3	44	1	15	1	10		
Art Director	1	15	1	10	1	8		
Announcers	2	26	1	8				
Public Relations Director and Staff	5	44	3	16	2	20		
TOTAL	22	327	11	138	7	77	2	20

Secretarial and Clerical								
TOTAL	18	90	12	60	4	20	1	5
Engineers [a]								
Studio (one shift)								
Video and Audio	6	72	5	55	2	18		
Projection, Film, Tape	5	60	4	44	1	9		
Maintenance	2	24	3	33	1	9		
Mobile	5	60					4	36
Broadcast and Control (two shifts)								
Master Control	2	24	2	22	2	18		
Film and Tape Broadcast	2	24	2	22	2	18		
Audio	2	24	2	22	2	18		
Extra for Weekends	—	20	—	18	—	15	—	15
TOTAL	24	308	18	216	10	105	4	51
Operations (studio and mobile)								
Supervisor	2	20	2	14	3	21		
Cameramen	14	140	9	63	1	7		
Lighting	3	30	3	21			2	10
Stagehands, Assistants, etc.	16	99	15	66	2	8		
TOTAL	35	289	29	164	6	36	2	10
Program Production (studio and mobile)								
Executive Producers	2	50	—	—	3	30		
Producers and Assistants	13	236	6	75				
Directors and Assistants	8	144	4	49	2	14		
Program Production Assistants	16	112	6	36				
TOTAL	39	542	16	160	5	44	—	—

Type of Station

	Key		Flag		Standard		Basic	
	Number	Total Salary (thousands of dollars)	Number	Total Salary (thousands of dollars)	Number	Total Salary (thousands of dollars)	Number	Total Salary (thousands of dollars)
Film Production Unit								
Producers, Directors, Assistants	6	94	3	33	}	}		
Research/Writers	2	30	1	10	3	24		
Editors and Assistants	6	62	2	14				
Camera, Lighting, Audio	3	35	2	16				
TOTAL	17	221	8	73	3	24	—	—
Scenic and Graphic (Total)	12	100	3	24	1	7		
Salary Supplements	—	97	—	65	—	20		
TOTAL PERSONNEL	167[a]	1,974	97	900	36	333	9	86

[a] Excluding engineers attendant at transmitter.
Source: Industrial consultants to the Commission

a state capital to be served by a standard station unless it fulfilled the conditions assumed for all the other cities, there would be 15 fewer standard stations, and 6 more basic stations and 9 more repeaters in the system, so that annual costs would be the less by another $7.5 million, or about $250 million.

Within the general framework of the model the factor of greatest uncertainty in the estimates is undoubtedly the question of what type of station any community will actually come to have. The estimates as they stand critically depend on the basic assumption that the goals of the Commission will come to be realized, and each representative station will be typical of the group of communities with the characteristics indicated in Table 1.

Station Costs

The estimated annual operating and capital costs, and the personnel and capital requirements of stations representative of each of the five types used in costing out the model are given in Tables 17, 18, and 19. These estimates were based on the operating experience and practice of both educational and commercial television. They attempt to portray the mode of operation and the corresponding costs of stations run well but economically.

In station operation in general, and in program production in particular, costs reflect not only the volume of output but more particularly the effort and attention devoted to the programs and, in the long run, the quality of the programs. Certain inputs, such as the services of broadcast control and transmitter engineers, require the same number of men per shift in standard, flag, and key stations, since the job to be done is the same for these activities in all three stations. On the other hand, a flag station requires about four times as many employees in program production teams and studio operation crews as does a standard station, and a key station seven times as many, even though the programming output of a key or flag station, measured in hours, is just about twice that of a standard station. Differences in station costs, accordingly, arise primarily from differences in the quality of the programming aimed at. A program is not necessarily better because it costs more, but it usually does cost more to do better programs. There is no particularly necessary cost of running a station, but there is a necessary cost of running it well. The estimated costs of the representative station of each type were based, essentially, on the consideration of what it would take to run a station of this type well.

Program Costs

The cost per hour of producing national programs is to be judged rather than estimated. That is to say, the cost depends fundamentally upon the level of quality sought. The judgment of national program quality embodied in the model is that the national programming to be obtained from the contract producers is to be the kind that costs about $45,000 an hour. The programming required from the key stations is to be the kind that costs about $30,000 an hour. While these costs are to be compared to costs of about $100,000 an hour for comparable programs produced for commercial networks,[7] they are from 50 to 100 percent higher than the average hourly costs of about $20,000 for the Public programs currently being produced for NET.

The difference in cost between the projected Public programs and the current ones proceeds partly from a difference in the program mix, a larger proportion of more costly programs such as dramas and documentaries having been included in the schedule projected for Public Television. It mainly represents, however, the greater amount of effort and attention to be given to each program, and the higher rate of payment to the creative talent involved in each program, both required for the proposed elevation of the standards of production of Public Television pro-

---

[7] An independent study by Arthur D. Little, Inc., of a recent season's new programs acquired by the national commercial networks indicated an average cost per hour of about $120,000. (Arthur D. Little, Inc., *Television Program Production Procurement and Syndication,* Cambridge, Massachusetts, February, 1966.) These costs of acquisition include producers' profits, so $100,000 an hour may be taken as a more conservative estimate of actual production costs.

grams. The largest single cost component of a national television program is the payment to the people who make the program. If the producers, writers, and actors are to spend more time with the program, and if they are to be people who can command higher pay, the program must cost more. The levels of cost, and the corresponding mode of operation for these programs were accordingly projected somewhere between the overly parsimonious current mode of production of educational television programs and the more elaborate styles of production and remuneration characteristic of commercial television. The mode of production priced here, it is believed, is that of a thoroughly professional production, but an economical one.

Table 20 shows the estimated composition of the costs of some Public Television programs that might be taken as representative of the 520 hours a year to be produced by the contract producers. These figures give some idea of where the money goes, and illustrate the wide range of variability even among programs of a given type, such as a documentary, but they are illustrative only. The fundamental basis of the estimated $23 million for contract programs must remain the twin judgments that ten hours a week are required, and that the kind of programming consistent with the cultural needs of the American people is the kind that costs $45,000 an hour.

The cost of national programs produced at key stations is included, in Table 3, in the costs of the stations. It has been separately estimated, however, and is shown in Table 21 and may be contrasted with the estimated costs of local and regional programs of key stations given in Table 22. The $30,000 per hour average for national programs produced at key stations again represents principally the judgment of the Commission and its staff that this is what the programming proposed for national distribution must cost if it is to do the job for which it is intended.

Indeed, the whole system's cost, estimated at $270 million annually, is a measure not of what educational television must cost in any absolute sense but of what it will cost if it is to do the job the Commission has set for it.

TABLE 20

REPRESENTATIVE COSTS OF 520 HOURS OF CONTRACT PROGRAMMING

Program Type [a]		Duration (hours per program)	Amount Produced (hours)	Crew and Facilities	Producer Team	Talent Etc.	Program Supplies	Over-head	Total	Cost Per Hour
						Costs per Program (thousands of dollars)				
Drama 1-hr.	(L)	1	13	9	14	40	20	17	100	100
Drama 2-hr.	(L)	2	26	14	21	60	30	25	150	75
Serial Drama	(F)	½	130	1	4	4	3	2.5	14.5	29
Light Entertainment	(L)	1	26	6	9	17	10	8	50	50
Children's	(F)	1	130	1	8	6	10	5	30	30
Adult Education	(L/F)	1	16	3	10	6	6	5	30	30
Documentaries	(F)									
Science		½	26	1	6	4	6	3	20	40
Historical		1	12	3	22	10	19	11	65	65
Humanities		1	12	2	16	7	13	7	45	45
Travel		1	12	2	16	7	17	8	50	50
Public Affairs										
Cost for ½ hr. programs										
Low		½	13	1	4	3	5	2	15	30
Medium		½	13	1	8	5	11	5	30	60
High		½	13	2	16	6	14	7	45	90
Cost for 1 hr. programs										
Low		1	26	2	12	5	10	6	35	35
Medium		1	26	3	24	10	21	12	70	70
High		1	26	5	36	14	32	18	105	105
			520							45 [b]

[a] (L)=Live/Tape Production; (F)=Film Production
[b] Average weighted in proportion to number of hours of each type produced per year.
Source: Industrial consultants to the Commission

TABLE 21

COSTS PER HOUR OF NATIONAL PROGRAMS
PRODUCED AT KEY STATIONS

	Mode of Production			
Cost Component	Studio (40 hrs/yr)	Mobile (8 hrs/yr)	Film (4 hrs/yr)	Average[a] (52 hrs/yr)
	(dollars per hour of programming)			
Crew and Facilities	4,750	3,750	2,000	4,400
Producer-Director Team	6,000	6,000	16,500	6,780
Talent and Fees	7,500	4,700	8,000	7,120
Program Supplies	6,750	4,300	11,000	6,700
Overhead (@ 20%)	5,000	3,750	7,500	5,000
TOTAL	30,000	22,500	45,000	30,000

[a] Weighted in proportion to number of hours produced in each mode per year.
Source: Industrial consultants to the Commission, guided by quality specifications for the programming furnished by the staff of the Commission

TABLE 22

COSTS PER HOUR OF LOCAL
AND EXCHANGE PROGRAMS
PRODUCED AT KEY STATIONS

	Mode of Production			
Cost Component	Studio (360 hrs/yr)	Mobile (129 hrs/yr)	Film (31 hrs/yr)	Average[a]
	(dollars per hour of programming)			
Crew and Facilities	1,600	1,438	387	1,580
Producer-Director Team	600	600	4,000	790
Talent and Fees	117	100	516	130
Program Supplies	200	200	1,000	250
Overhead (@ 20%)	503	566	1,194	550
TOTAL	3,020	3,404	7,097	3,300

[a] Weighted in proportion to number of hours of each type produced per year.
Source: Industrial consultants to the Commission

TECHNOLOGY AND TELEVISION
by Albert G. Hill

Dr. Hill is Professor of Physics, Massachusetts Institute of Technology.

Technological progress which will affect television in the future falls into two general categories: electronics and new materials. Improvements in electronics for enhancing the quality of television presentation and the better distribution of television signals can be predicted fairly well. Progress in materials research is much more difficult to predict. The reason for this difference is simply that the understanding of electronics and electromagnetic techniques is very deep, and breakthroughs in basic principles are unlikely. In contrast, our understanding of materials is really in its infancy and the field is still wide open for very major advances.

In the near future, five to ten years from now, we can predict with a good degree of reliability certain advances in television technology based on new and improved electronic techniques because of our thoroughgoing understanding of basic electromagnetic phenomena. In the less certain area of improved materials, predictions for the near future are much less credible. In the more distant future of ten to twenty years, one can anticipate with certainty a number of major changes, but the precise form these changes may take is not predictable because of our lack of fundamental knowledge of materials.

Technology *by itself* can, in the near future, produce less expensive network facilities than the present landlines, can produce less expensive and more readily usable storage devices, can make for small improvements in set quality, and can make better access to homes via coaxial cable than presently exists. However, technology, when used by wise management and applied to the entire problem, can make tremendous improvements in both commercial and noncommercial television. In addition, technology can aid the program creators and have a real influence in improving program content. Improvement of program content of educational television and its nationwide distribution by economical means now possible will make the cost per viewer of educational television more in keeping with that of commercial television.

Satellites

The transmission of television signals across oceans is economically possible only by the use of satellites, and will probably remain so. The use of satellites for the transmission of public television signals in this country is only warranted if the economics are favorable and if the necessary frequency allocation is possible. Present satellite technology indicates that in the term of two to five years the networking of educational television stations can probably be done for about half the overall price of the present landline systems, provided the switching requirements are kept simple. Such a system would enable the establishment of a network with ten to twenty transmitting stations and a receiving station at every educational television broadcast station.

With the present development underway by the National Aeronautics and Space Administration of large boosters for our national space program, the realization of a multichannel system for television distribution is possible in the next five to seven years. By the proper design of satellites transmitting more power than present satellites, the ground receiving stations can be made to cost no more than $35,000 and a lower overall system cost is possible. Ground transmitting stations would cost on the order of $150,000. Such a system would allow the distribution of television signals from, say, fifteen regions of the country to any television station which cares to install a relatively inexpensive receiver, and at a cost of no more than half the present landline cost.

In the next two to three years it would be quite feasible

as an experimental program to position a synchronous satellite of modest design requirements with the equivalent capacity of two television channels. The cost could well be justified on the basis of the wealth of experience brought to Public Television service by this simple approach to the network problem, and by a variety of measurements such as an investigation of the interference produced by satellites radiating at many different frequencies. The limitation on the number of channels available for satellite transmission in the future will be imposed entirely by the need for conservation of the very precious frequency spectrum, and not by the cost of satellites and their associated ground equipment.

Technically it is possible to achieve direct broadcasting to the home or to schools from satellites in the next ten years. In countries which have no such land networks as the very complicated and extensive one of the United States, this might be a solution to some of their problems such as classroom instruction. In the United States, where our ability to transfer television signals from almost any part of the country to any other is already extensive, it is hard to see that there is any economic advantage to broadcasting directly to the home, since new home antennas would be required. In addition, any satellite-to-home system would bypass and hence make obsolete our local stations and undoubtedly would neglect local and sectional interests.

Other Long-Distance Distribution Systems

Our present network television is carried throughout the country by line-of-sight microwave systems, and although normal improvements in these systems will reduce the cost somewhat, the chances are that additional capacity of this type will be more expensive than satellite systems for near-transcontinental hops. There are now under development, but still some way from fruition, other types of high-capacity signal distribution systems which will be economically competitive with the present microwave system and might become competitive with satellite systems. Apart from economics, these systems will confine the electromagnetic carriers so that there will be no interference whatever with other systems, and hence they will not be limited by frequency considerations.

Even the present microwave line-of-sight systems are susceptible to interference produced by other signals, and hence the new system will provide for signal distribution unlimited by any factors except economic ones.

Storage

High-quality storage of television signals is now an accepted fact and is used constantly by commercial stations. This storage is in general used only for short times for re-broadcast purposes. Long-time storage by present methods is too bulky and too expensive. Industry is developing new systems which show great promise but presently are considered proprietary.

We forecast that within five years there will be available new video capabilities with storage devices of cost and bulk more suitable for indefinite storage. This device, or these devices, will bear to visual reproduction the same relation that LP records bear to audio reproduction and at not too different a cost.

The combination of a satellite channel with standby, serving educational television, plus high-quality tapes for reproduction of live programs and the new low-cost video storage device will make for an extremely flexible educational television system. In purely instructional television, the classroom teacher will no longer be tied to the hours of broadcast of the local educational station, but will be able to select tapes from a library in the same way records or books are selected today.

Color film with sound track is still the best means for high-quality storage and may well remain so. The problem with film has always been the development of an easy-to-load and inexpensive projection device. Because of the widespread and growing use of television for instructional purposes in the classroom, the development of inexpensive television storage devices is very important. However, in many uses, especially where fine-grain presentation is de-

sired, there exists a need for an inexpensive sound film pro-
jector of the cartridge-loading type for individual or small
class use.

Cables for Home Reception

For a number of years cable-antenna television systems
(community antenna television systems) have been available to isolated communities unable to receive directly
broadcast signals, to bring television programs into the
home with a reasonable monthly charge of about five dollars. These systems have also spread to densely populated
cities such as New York, where manmade structures have
interfered with the reception of broadcast signals. With
cables becoming more and more available to the home, the
possibility of their more widespread use must be considered.

Signals over cables, while limited to the same frequency
spectrum as broadcast signals, do not interfere with other
signals outside the cable, so channels reserved for services
other than broadcast television can be used by the cable.

With not too expensive additions to present and future
cable systems, it should be quite possible to put twenty
television channels on a cable, and these could be received
by present all-channel receivers.

Sound

Sound, as broadcast, is of very high quality; sound as
reproduced by the set is of very low quality because of the
present set speakers. For a very few cents at the factory,
an access jack could be provided to tie the high-quality
sound signal to high-fidelity reception equipment at the
owner's option.

The Distant Future

In the period of ten to twenty-five years from now one
can readily imagine many homes which contain a sophisticated communications center. With only modest improvements in cables and television sets, as many as eighty-two
television channels or their equivalent could be available in
the home for a wide variety of services. These might include:

a. The normal television broadcast channels.

b. Special channels reserved for the various performing arts, i.e., separate channels for drama, opera, ballet, and symphonic or chamber music.

c. Several channels of live broadcasts of the theater, movies, sporting events, and other entertainment which would undoubtedly require a fee on a subscription basis.

d. News, weather, time, and other repetitive services.

e. Shopping services, carried in a manner similar to daily newspaper advertising and the Yellow Page type of advertising.

f. Library services, which will allow the distribution of requested library information in the form of facsimile.

g. Picture phones.

For laboratory and office use, random access to centralized computer services and intercomputer exchange between research computers are feasible now. The growth of these services will be extraordinary.

With the ability to have present in the home or office the equivalent of eighty-two television channels with a variety of information carried, it is apparent that the consumer's needs can be met in ways not imagined here. As such systems become available, new uses will undoubtedly be found.

For most of the applications mentioned the communication is one-way to the home. However for many of the services, such as the shopping service, it would be desirable to be able to signal to the program originator such things as an intention to buy a certain item or an inquiry as to its price or expected service life. Here a simple coded type of inquiry from the home could readily be added to make the responses automatic.

There are other characteristics of television that future technology can bring if the demand is there. Such developments as three-dimensional television, very fine-grained television for special purposes, very fine gradation of light, shadow and color — all of these are possible. Besides some development work, they require more bandwidth and more money. One can almost say that within the limits of the concept of transmitted picture and sound, anything is technically possible.

Improvements in Television Sets

The present design of television sets and the standards of both black-and-white and color transmission and reproduction were essentially developed in the period from 1946 to 1952. In a broad sense this was our first attempt, and by and large for the time period it was a very good one. However a decade and a half of research and development have gone by with no improvement in the quality of television. Any such improvement would probably require a change of standards, but these standards are tied up to some 60 million television sets.

Any change in standards, no matter how valuable, which makes obsolete some 60 million television sets is not only extraordinarily expensive but also most unpopular. However, the longer we postpone any change of standards, the more certain we are to become tied to the technology of 1949. We will be in the same position vis-a-vis television standards in a few more years that we are now in with regard to changing our basic measurements to the metric system. While the point of no return may have been reached with regard to the English system of measurements, we have not yet reached that point with television. But immediate action is required regarding the use of the frequency spectrum.

Changes and improvements in television technology since the start of broadcasting have been governed entirely by the marketplace. The market is large and important and cannot change by itself without adversely affecting the tremendous investment. Although the technology applied to present-day television resides almost entirely in industry, the know-how is completely open to all technologists. Industrial technology is capable of making improvements, but it is difficult for industry alone to take a bold step in changing standards.

Frequency Use and Conservation

At the present time we have a completely filled VHF band and a rapidly filling UHF band. However, we note that the overwhelming majority of all man-hours of viewing are spent with sets tuned to the VHF band. It is therefore possible, at relatively small cost and dislocation, to reserve part of the UHF band for experimental purposes in research for better quality.

Although the gross national product continues to increase and items which require only more dollars for improvement can be anticipated with time, the use of the natural frequency spectrum is another matter. There is only so much of it, and any waste must be carefully prevented. It is true that there are underway applied research programs seeking to broadcast with a smaller portion of the spectrum while transmitting the same amount of video information. These developments are extraordinarily important but will not come to fruition for at least ten years and probably a great deal more.

It is to be hoped that the precious UHF spectrum can be allocated grudgingly to insure that the best possible use of television with improved quality of picture transmission is a firm requirement. The present standards must be tied to the VHF band in order to protect the interests of the public and of industry, but a part of the UHF band should be opened for experimentation and improvement.

While we may expect greater use of cables, it must be remembered that the broadcast receiver is the least expensive method of getting a television signal into the home and is the only method economically possible for a large fraction of television viewers.

Televistas: Looking Ahead Through Side Windows

by J. C. R. Licklider

Dr. Licklider is Consultant to the IBM Director of Research and Visiting Professor at the Massachusetts Institute of Technology.

Previously Lecturer in Psychology at Harvard, Associate Professor of Psychology and Communications at Massachusetts Institute of Technology, Vice President of Bolt Beranek and Newman, Inc., and Director for Behavioral Sciences and Information Processing Research of the Advanced Research Projects Agency, Department of Defense.

In planning to improve the use of television for educational purposes, most people have accepted the basic framework of conventional broadcast television.* That framework determines the basic structure of their thinking and in the process delimits it. For example, a person who thinks of educational television as a set of educational functions supported by the framework of conventional broadcast television is unlikely to think of television as a medium for two-way communication or as a way of transmitting the text of a book or the stimulus material for a course of programmed instruction.

The main purpose of this paper is to explore some of the possibilities that come to mind when one deliberately looks aside from the central line of thought about educational television and rejects the assumption that educational applications have to be built upon the framework of conventional broadcast television. It is not part of the purpose to argue that what is to be seen out the "side windows" is

*The term "broadcast," as I use it here, is not intended to imply that signals are necessarily radiated into space from an antenna. If a program were sent out to the public through coaxial cables, the program would be "broadcast."

more attractive than the view along the central path. The intention is merely to examine briefly a collection of ideas that seem interesting from a technical point of view and to consider how they might fit into the future of education supported by technology. It seems important to do this because the modern technology of information and communications is opening up a wide horizon of bright prospects, most of which seem to be technically achievable. These prospects should be held in mind, and brought into active interplay with pedagogical, psychological, economic, and philosophical factors, during this crucial period of planning and deciding the course of educational television.

"INTERACTIVE" AND "SELECTIVE" TELEVISION

The great simplifying characteristics of conventional broadcast television are that it is broadcast and that the broadcast stations transmit to viewers who do not transmit back. Under past technological constraints, those characteristics were a *sine qua non* for a wide-band medium. That is to say, to justify the use of a medium capable of carrying a very large amount of information each second, one had to reach a mass audience and therefore could not provide channels through which the many individual members of a large audience could talk back. In the future, technology will constrain less severely. We should therefore think about what educational television might do and what it might achieve if it could afford to present a much wider range of programs, direct its services to small and highly selected audiences, and even engage in two-way communication.

From an educator's point of view, the main intrinsic defects of broadcast television are that it offers everyone the same thing and does not give its viewers a direct way of participating in its programs or interacting with its program material. It is likely that advances in technological capability and changes in social perspective will multiply the channels available to educational television, making it possible for educational television to offer a wide variety of programs and services to meet diverse educational needs selectively and responsively. Indeed, it is possible that facilities will become available to educational television that will permit people to participate directly in educational programs and to interact directly with subject matter. These possibilities evoke concepts that I shall call "selective television" and "interactive television." Since interaction is such a strong factor in learning, let us consider it first.

Interactive Participation

Viewers do, in a sense, participate in conventional television programs. If the program material is dramatic and matched to a viewer's motivations, the viewer may sit on the edge of his chair, empathize overtly, and utter words of encouragement. That kind of participation fails, however, to qualify as *inter*active participation, since the actual course of a broadcast television program depends in no way upon the concurrent behavior of its viewers. The criterion for what is here called "interaction" is that both the program and the viewer be capable of influencing each other.

From a psychologist's point of view, there is an important difference between interactive and noninteractive participation which is crucial to the development, as distinguished from the exploitation, of motivation. Noninteractive participation stems from previously established drives, but it does not contribute effectively to the development or augmentation of motivation. Interactive participation, on the other hand, is regenerative. It stems from already established motivation and may in turn strengthen and even restructure that motivation.

It is obvious enough how viewers can react to a television program, but how can a television program react to its viewers? If it is a set piece, it can do nothing that is not set into it. If it is a contingent program, on the other hand, it can in principle adapt itself to its audience as a lecturer adapts himself to his. Indeed, if the "program" is an array of contingent programs — a "multiple-track" program, in the parlance of programmed instruction — it can adjust itself simultaneously in different ways to achieve and maintain resonance with each of several or many sectors of its overall audience. The trouble, of course, is that the difficulty of selective adjustment increases with the size of the audience. Obviously, there is an essential incompatibility between viewer-program interaction and mass media.

Participating by Selecting

For a viewer of educational television, the next best thing to having the program itself react to him may be to select from an ensemble of transmitted alternatives the one that is most appropriate to his needs or interests. The viewer of conventional television can, of course, select a channel and change his selection whenever he likes. That is good as far as it goes, but it does not go far enough to give the viewer any sense of participation in a program. The idea of "participating by selecting" involves the assumption that broader and more systematically organized sets of options can be offered to the viewer and that more convenient and more sophisticated ways of selecting among the options can be provided.

On *a priori* grounds, to augment the selectability of program material seems less likely to open significant new opportunities than does the establishment of true interaction between the viewer and the program itself. However, selectability does not suffer as severely the essential incompatibility with mass-audience broadcasting that handicaps interaction, since the entire process of selecting can be carried out at the receiver and no feedback channel from the home to the television station is required. Let us, therefore, consider a few approaches that involve selection by the viewer — approaches that might achieve some of the same advantages as interaction without giving up mass audiences.

SELECTIVE BROADCAST TELEVISION

The approach to improving the effectiveness of educational television that requires the least modification of the framework of conventional broadcast television is one that takes advantage of increased availability of television channels to broadcast a large amount of carefully scheduled and coordinated material, from which individual viewers can select what meets their needs and interests. Each broadcast program, for example, could be an array of subprograms, from which each viewer could select one. From time to time, either at specified points in the program or at moments of his own choosing, the viewer could switch from one subprogram to another. A few of the ways in which this general method could be applied are suggested by the following ideas:

1.   Several cameras are used to cover a group discussion, a play, or a football game. All the signals are broadcast and received by the television receiver. Associated with each receiving set is a control by means of which the viewer selects the camera through which he wishes to watch.

2.   The picture of a work of art or of a scene on a large stage is transmitted in such a way as to preserve very fine detail. A control on the receiver permits the viewer to select whatever part he likes of the overall picture for display upon his screen. Having mastered the control arrangement, the viewer can let his eyes explore a painting almost as though he were before it in the gallery or follow spontaneously the action of a dynamic scene.

3.   The news broadcast has two main parts. First there is a summary in which the essence of each item is presented very briefly. During this presentation, the viewer presses a button each time he sees or hears something he wants to learn more about. Then, during the second part of the broadcast, when fuller and more penetrating accounts are given of the various developments, his receiver selects for

him and presents to him a program custom tailored to his interests.

4. Instead of broadcasting a "moving picture" — a succession of still pictures, each minutely different from its predecessor — the transmitter sends out a sequence of still pictures in which one is quite independent of the next. The still pictures, coming at a rate of thirty per second, constitute a vast informational resource from which each receiver can select. The receivers are designed to pick out certain images and to hold each one for view until its selected successor arrives. Thus the viewer sees a succession of still pictures, each selected from a large set of alternatives.

The first two schemes would be interesting only if means were developed through which viewers could control the selection and display of received images very conveniently and very naturally, almost as a part of the act of viewing. The third scheme does not appear to involve any problems of adjustment by the viewer that would require the development of sophisticated means, but it does invite development of sophisticated arrangements for controlling the selection of program elements on the basis of the viewer's pattern of interests and preferences. The basic idea, suggested in terms of an augmented newscast, was to offer a variety of program elements, transmitting them in several parallel sequences so that each viewer's receiving set could make its own selection. If the entire schedule of offerings were preannounced, each viewer might of course piece together his own news program by operating a simple channel selector. To make the scheme practicable, however, it would be necessary to provide, for each receiver, a programmable selection controller. This notion, which tends to develop itself into a concept that might be called the "control subsystem" of the home information system, will be pertinent also to other ideas to be introduced later.

Assuming a sophisticated control subsystem, one can envisage application of "custom tailoring" to other things than news. It would be especially appropriate for announcements of forthcoming events and, indeed, for any subject matter that naturally divides itself into elements of which some are likely to be of interest to one viewer and others to another. Inasmuch as materials and services offered for sale to the public constitute precisely such a subject matter — and the development of sophisticated control subsystems would open new fields of advertising for commercial television — one can look forward to the actual appearance in the home of such selective means as we have been envisioning.

In the fourth scheme, many sequences can be carried by a single television channel of normal bandwidth because they are sequences of images separated by seconds of time rather than by milliseconds. The basic idea — not very appealing on first thought — is to give up the motion-picture quality of conventional television in order to make room for the many alternatives demanded for certain applications of selective television. If for each viewer there were one image every ten seconds, on the average, instead of thirty images every second as in conventional television, the same channel that carries a conventional moving television picture could carry three hundred entirely different sequences of images. Selecting from those three hundred sequences, each home television receiver could assemble its own unique program.

If the images had to be selected deliberately by the viewer, through some explicit control action taken each time he wanted to see a new picture, the idea of trading the dynamic motion-picture quality of conventional television for the high degree of selectability under discussion probably would not seem attractive for any purpose. However, if we recall and extend the concept of a control subsystem introduced earlier, we see that the viewer need not concern himself with the individual selections. The procedure governing the selections can be programmed into the control subsystem and, what is most important, the procedure can be made contingent upon relations between the viewer's responses and criteria transmitted along with the sequences of pictures. This notion of making the selection of the next picture contingent upon the viewer's responses to preceding pictures — responses he might make by pointing to part of the picture with a stylus or by pressing buttons on a portable response unit — can, in effect, convert television into a radically different and very interesting new medium.

The new medium would be especially appropriate for programmed instruction. Each receiving set would be equipped with a "light pointer" (a stylus connected to the receiver in such a way as to communicate the viewer's responses to the control subsystem), and scoring criteria would be transmitted along with the picture and sound of each "frame" of instruction. The result would be an extremely sophisticated teaching machine capable of presenting self-scoring multi-track instructional programs with automatic path selection. With such a medium, and with the aid of sophisticated programming, one should be able to involve each individual "telestudent" in an active participation that would verge upon true interaction with the program material.

Any scheme that requires the television receiver to hold an image for several seconds requires a receiver somewhat different from conventional receivers that use short-persistence picture tubes and embody no other means for storing the image than is inherent in the luminous phosphor of the display screen. However, devices and techniques now under development offer hope that receivers of the kind we have been discussing will be technically and economically feasible within a few years. Several different "buffer storage" devices have been tested successfully, and storage tubes are available that will hold their images until deliberately erased. An early development version of a "meshless" storage tube capable of displaying pictures with high resolution (i.e., the reproduction of fine detail) was demonstrated recently.

The dynamic — or, to put it more precisely, the kinematic — quality of moving pictures and conventional television is so obviously valuable that the thought of sacrificing it to achieve some other quality, such as the selectability just discussed, is likely to require a considerable amount of urging, even though assurance be given that the idea is to supplement rather to replace the standard medium. But it is important to keep the mind open to periodic reassessment of the values and costs of various ways of using the resources available to television. It is important to face the fact that the cost of the kinematic quality is high. Another costly quality is what we might call the "full-pictorial" quality of the conventional television image. Conventional television does not provide very high resolution, but it does reproduce more or less faithfully the hue, the saturation, and the brightness of each small area of the scene before the camera. Typically, there is a large amount of information in a detailed picture, and it takes a wide channel to transmit such a picture in a short time. With the facilities required to transmit one image of full-pictorial quality, one could transmit many pages of letters and numbers or many line diagrams, graphs, and sketches. Text and line drawings can of course be transmitted, received, and displayed either with motion or without.

Recorded Television

The development of low-cost video recorders and recordings adds important new dimensions to educational television. The impact of these components will depend upon the quality and reliability of their performance, upon their cost, upon the merit of the programs available to and through them, and upon the effectiveness of the program distribution systems. The potential seems very great, for it includes both a marked increase in the number of programs from which viewers may select and freedom from the constraint of having to synchronize the viewers' schedules with the broadcasters'.

"Hard-Copy" Television

Although we are used to thinking of the output of a television set as ephemeral pictures ("soft copy") and sound, it is interesting to consider also some of the possibilities and problems suggested by the phrase "hard-copy television." The change of domain from soft copy to hard requires that we make a corresponding change in the range of functions considered. Perhaps the most appropriate functions for hard-copy television overlap the functions now served by newspapers and magazines.

The concept of the newspaper delivered by wire has been discussed widely enough to need no elaboration here, but it may be worthwhile to relate it to ideas presented earlier about selection of program material by the viewer. The essential things are to give the viewer a way of specifying what he wants to have put into his newspaper and to incorporate into his receiver the means for selecting and recording, and later playing back upon demand, the appropriate items. Those requirements can be met by a blend of "ordering from menu" (as suggested earlier in connection with the augmented newscast) and "matching to profile" (as used in systems for selective dissemination of information). In one approach, for example, the televised newspaper would periodically broadcast an index to forthcoming news items, on the basis of which "subscribers" would make selections and designate them to the control sections of their receiving sets. Each control section would add to the list of designated selections a list of calculated selections, the latter being arrived at by comparing viewers' expressed interests with available news items. (The calculating might be done by a multiple-access computing service and fed into the receiving set via telephone lines. Indeed, the control section of the receiving set might reside mainly or even exclusively in a central computer somewhere.) The receiving set would then copy the desired items "off the air" and present them in the form of a custommade family newspaper or custom-made newspapers for individual members of the family.

The basic theme of the foregoing discussion is of course selectivity, and the basic problem is the one already encountered and discussed: the problem of broadcasting enough alternatives to provide a basis for truly sharp selection. It is important to note how much that problem is simplified by the switch from the moving pictures of conventional television to the mainly alphabetic text of the news article. The amount of space in the frequency spectrum (a bandwidth of about 5 million Hertz) required to transmit a conventional television program will carry about a million alphanumeric characters (letters, numbers, punctuation marks, etc.) per second. A standard newspaper column of text contains about four thousand characters. Thus one conventional television channel could carry the alphanumeric contents of a thirty-page newspaper each second. Indeed, if a recent estimate is even approximately correct, one television channel could transmit — on a continuing basis, as it is published — every bit of text that is published in any newspaper, magazine, journal, or book that finds its way into any recognized library or document room in the world. (J. W. Senders's estimate in 1963 was about two million bits per second.*) Evidently, if we limit the discourse to alphanumeric text, it is not lack of bandwidth that stands in the way of offering the world's fund of news and knowledge to every man in his own home.

All the news may fall within it, but not all the world's fund of knowledge falls properly within the domain — even within the here considerably extended domain — of broadcast media. The categories of content that do seem worth considering include, in addition to news, all the schedules and advance announcements and all the background information and evaluative commentary that pertain to situations or events of widespread interest, for no other medium than television has the potential capacity and selectivity to make available to each person at the time and place of his choosing his own self-prescribed subset of the whole.

Balance

In the foregoing sections, we have examined several possible variations of broadcast television, ranging from high-resolution motion pictures, with viewer control of the field of view, to hard-copy alphanumeric text. Although we examined them separately, we should think of them as components that technology could make available for use in a coherent communication system. In communicat-

*See *Science*, Vol. 141 (1963), pp. 1067–1068.

ing the news, there is a place for live color and motion coverage, another place for text, and still other places for most of the other variations. During a performance by a symphony orchestra, the main need is for high-quality sound and good pictures, but before and after the performance some of the other variations would find roles to play — especially if the viewer's purpose included learning as well as enjoying.

INTERACTIVE "NARROWCAST" TELEVISION

The ideas discussed in the previous section suffered from the conflict between the effort to select material of interest to the individual and the commitment to broadcast to a mass audience. Indeed, the central concept of "interaction" had to be set aside (except insofar as interaction could be simulated through schemes based on selection) because broadcasting to a mass audience essentially precludes interaction.

Networks for Narrowcasting

For educational television, a basic and important question is whether to continue to plan in terms of broadcasting to a mass audience or to adopt a framework in which the overall audience divides itself into many subsets and communication with each subset is carried through its own channel or channels. In the latter case, educational television would be pluralistic operationally and technologically as well as philosophically, offering a multiplicity of programs, services, and techniques, and using a multiplicity of channels.

Here I should like to coin the term "narrowcasting," using it to emphasize the rejection or dissolution of the constraints imposed by commitment to a monolithic mass-appeal, broadcast approach. I do not mean to imply that educational television has been wholly dedicated to such an approach or such a philosophy; indeed, I recognize that educational television stations have for many years carried programs designed for narrow sectors of the public. Narrowcasting, however, may suggest more efficient procedures than broadcasting throughout a wide area in order to reach a small, select audience, and it is meant to imply not only that the subject matter is designed to appeal to selected groups but also that the distribution channels are so arranged as to carry each program or service to its proper audience.

Although broadcasting throughout an area from a transmitting antenna to many receiving antennas is by no means ruled out of the picture, linear channels — channels consisting of coaxial cables or wave guides or microwave links — seem in principle to be better suited to the purpose of carrying messages to selected audiences. Wide-band linear communications channels will be expensive, but much less expensive than transportation channels. For the purposes of this section, let us make the assumptions (1) that in the near term educational television gets a large number of additional channels of some kind* and (2) that in the long term it has access to such a network as one can imagine by projecting and augmenting the development of community-antenna television. The cables of CATV will evolve into multipurpose local networks, and the local networks will be linked together to form regional, national, and even international networks. The linking may involve broadcast transmission, with satellite relays playing an important role, and it may involve additional cables, wave guides, microwave channels, and so on.

The CATV networks that have recently come into the limelight are of course unidirectional. Supplementary facilities are required to permit communication from the home back to the station. Fortunately, the supplementary channels need not be wide-band channels. For some "feedback" purposes, the existing telephone system is suitable, but it is not designed to function with a large fraction of its terminals and peripheral lines in use at the same time. Perhaps very simple transmitters can be devised that will

*UHF channels, microwave channels, channels made feasible by satellite relays, etc.

make it possible to use coaxial cables for "feedback" as well as "outward" signaling. If that should turn out not to be technically practicable and no alternative capable of serving the feedback function were made available, I think we could be correctly accused of having a blind spot in our foresight. What more appropriate contribution could technology make to democracy than good channels of communication directed from every man to the foci of the society?

In present-day CATV, the aim (only slightly oversimplified) is to connect as many homes as possible through one cable to one antenna station. The network for narrowcasting, however, should approach as closely as is economically possible — which for a time may not be very closely — the ideal of a private cable to every home. The compromise I have in mind is one in which the quasi-geographical hierarchy of governmental and political organization, down to the level of neighborhoods, is reflected in a flexible organization of the network. That would provide a basis for effective selection of audiences at any local, regional, or national level in support of society-wide functions, such as government, education, and supply, that are organized mainly upon a geographical framework. Special functions not so organized, and not of wide enough interest to warrant being made available to everyone at his own property line, are served by main channels that extend as far as local tapping points, where connections are made to local cables owned by or leased or charged to individual subscribers.

Consider, now, the problem of achieving high educational purposes — and of being effective throughout the socioeconomic range as well as across the geographical span of the nation — with the help of such transmission facilities as we have just assumed. What can we hope to do when the bandwidth constraint is loosened?

Functions and Services

Based on a philosophy that appreciates the interaction value of diversity among the personalities, attitudes, and interest patterns of individuals as well as the cohesion value of community in language and cultural heritage — and a philosophy that prefers active participation to passive observation — narrowcast television would endeavor not merely to present programs of general interest but to fulfill functions and provide services of special interest to groups of medium and even small size. The standard television functions would grow deeper roots: The news would include neighborhood and community news as well as regional, national, and international. The high-school football game and the local tennis finals as well as the bowl games and national championships would be on television. Community theater would have a chance to compete, if not with Broadway, with Hollywood. Extension of such functions to the local level might promote not only the personal involvement of viewers in the programs but also the participation of many people outside professional television in the preparation and presentation of television programs.

In the fields of government and politics, the impact of narrowcasting might be profound. Town meetings could be not merely televised but *held* via television. Every representative at every level of government could report periodically to his constituency. Every administrative official could explain the objectives of his agency and the significance of his executive actions. Every candidate could count on opportunities to reach the voters "live," and every voter could expect to see and hear live candidates under circumstances that would let him see through the "images" into the men.

In the performing arts, narrowcasting would probably do more for performers than for audiences. It would provide to many more performers the opportunity to have an audience and to profit from audience reaction. It would introduce a new factor into the dynamics of community theater. Especially at community and regional levels, performing artists make excellent audiences for other performing artists. Putting that fact together with the availability of links connecting local and regional networks suggests that narrowcast television might serve the performing arts best by permitting the members of community groups all over the country to see and hear one another in action — symphony musicians communicating with symphony musicians, dancers with dancers, actors with actors, and so on. Thus facilitated, and with local, regional, and national lay audiences potentially available to them, the performing arts might burgeon like Australian tennis.

In the fine arts, narrowcasting could bring all the nation's, perhaps even much of the world's, great treasures into the home. Educational television would continue, of course, to present visits to the great museums under the guidance and with the commentary of distinguished authorities, and it would continue to present courses in history and appreciation of art. However, it would not stop there. Every museum would have a camera, lights, and connections to the network. In data bases accessible through the network, the inventories of all the museums would be held. With the assistance of a group of its members, or perhaps with the cooperation of an art school, each museum would feed into the network, according to schedules and directions arranged with programming offices, images of its works of art. The requests might originate either with official television agencies or with informal groups of viewers such as art clubs, or even with individual viewers. This approach would put some of the initiative for programming into the hands of groups outside professional television.

All the professions are concerned with continuing education of their members, in which narrowcast television could play an important role, and all have responsibilities to their publics, to which narrowcast television could provide selective channels. For science and engineering, indeed, narrowcasting might offer the first promising approach to the problem of educating the general public to comprehend the social impact of technology.

Finally, we come to the two fields in which nonconventional television appears to offer the clearest promises: the field of the library and the field of deliberate teaching and learning. The promises are offered jointly by narrowcast television and intercommunicational television. Let us consider here a few ideas pertinent to the former.

Narrowcast Television and Libraries

The community libraries suffer from a difficulty that is very familiar to broadcast television: economic considerations make it impracticable to offer much that is not sure to appeal to a large audience. In the case of the libraries the trouble stems from the fact that the distribution procedure is set up backwards, so to speak. First, many copies of each book are produced. Then the books are stored near where they may be wanted. And finally, prospective users go to nearby repositories, make requests, and, if the books requested are available there, borrow the books, read them, and return them. The economic disadvantages of duplicating, distributing, and storing books that may never be read is obvious. Some of the techniques of what is currently known as the "non-Gutenberg technology" make it possible to avoid most of that disadvantage.

Modern library science and technology deal, of course, with other problems than physical access to specified books. In the scientist's and engineer's use of the library, and probably also in most of the uses that arise in everyman's everyday life, the basic objective is not a document but the answer to a question or the solution to a problem. Even if the user is constrained (by the partly technical and partly economic infeasibility of automatic question answerers and problem solvers) from demanding direct access to his basic objective, he needs as much help in finding out which documents to ask for as he does in obtaining copies of the documents he requests. Fortunately, documentation experts are making fair progress in mastering the process of finding documents pertinent to a given request. The techniques — which include augmented cataloguing, deep subject-matter indexing, citation indexing and "bibliographic coupling" through citations, matching of profiles and prescriptions, and of course abstracting — require trained people, programmed computers, and a steady work load. They are, as the library system is currently organized, beyond the means of most community (and indeed many other) libraries.

Narrowcast television fits neatly into an obvious solution of the problem just posed. Master copies of documents are held at central repositories: a national archive for infrequently used items, regional centers for moderately active items, and so on. All the libraries and document centers are netted together, and many of the nodes of their network communicate with nodes of the educational television network — and of course with nodes of other networks serving governmental agencies, universities, and business and industry. To use the library from his home, a person would communicate with a local station of the library network, through either his telephone or a feedback channel associated with his home information center, and describe his request to a person (perhaps eventually to a machine) at the station. The contents of the specified documents would be read automatically from the masters. The control system of the requester's home information center would be notified of the scheduled transmission time. At the designated time, the information would flow from the library's buffer memory through wide-band channels into the television network and thence to the automatically readied receiving set and recorder. Finally, the requester would play the record back through his display subsystem and study the documents at his leisure.

Many technical problems would arise in the development of such a system. Yet almost everyone agrees that they could be solved. And, as mentioned, progress on the "intellectual" problems of retrieval and dissemination is promising enough to encourage anticipation of some kind of matching of library and television within the next two decades. The main justifications for adopting a skeptical attitude are economic. Most of the functions envisaged require sophisticated equipment at the receiving location. There is little doubt that, if it were guaranteed a mass market, American industry would quickly develop the capability of manufacturing the sophisticated equipment at low cost. However, the economics of advanced home information systems will probably suffer, as the economics of conventional broadcast television did in its early days, from a chicken-and-egg dilemma. The needed equipment would be inexpensive if there were a mass market, and there would be a mass market if the needed equipment were inexpensive, but since neither antecedent prevails, neither consequence follows. To anyone who thinks he sees in technology's potential armamentarium the weapons that can win the war against poverty — or even battles against delinquency or unskilledness — the inhibitory effect of that modest mixture of logic and economics is likely to be most frustrating.

Instructional Television

The concept of narrowcasting makes room for — and indeed calls for — great extension and augmentation of instructional television. The thing that, in my assessment, offers the most credible promise of making deliberate instruction and deliberate study attractive to almost everyone is a combination of inspiration through exposure to great minds and reinforcement through interaction with a rich and well-programmed base of information under the aegis of a skilled tutor. (I use the term "reinforcement" in the sense developed by Skinnerian psychologists, and I have in mind an awareness, derived from experience with computer-assisted instruction, that motivation is strengthened and learning fostered almost magically by close interaction with a partner that presents precisely appropriate answers, acknowledgments, rewards, and even punishments at precisely the right times. Indeed, a large part of the skilled tutoring will doubtless be done, in future educational systems, by programmed digital computers.)

The central idea to be developed under the heading of instructional television, then, is the idea of using augmented television facilities in an all-out effort to provide a self-motivating, self-rewarding kind of educational opportunity on a wide scale. The effort would of course have to be coordinated with schools and colleges. Indeed, it would have to involve a considerable fraction of the intellectual resources of the country.

Most of the ideas about devices and techniques that

have been mentioned are pertinent to the development of coherent systems to facilitate instruction and learning. Color motion pictures will be vital because they can convey into the home the personalities of distinguished men and the dynamic performances of skilled lecturers, and because they can show how intricate things work. The televised library will play an important role because it will be responsive to, and will foster, initiative on the part of the student. However, the basic task of instructing — of building structures of knowledge within the minds of students and training into their nervous systems the skills required in adjustment to modern life — will fall upon instructional programs with which students can interact.

The major technical question, I think, is how much interaction between students and contingently adapting and responding instructional programs can be accomplished through narrowcast television. Such programs will rely heavily upon transmission schemes of the kind described earlier as offering to each viewer a wide selection of lantern-slide sequences with audio accompaniment. It may turn out that sufficiently dynamic interaction with each one of many students can be achieved within the framework of the scheme in which the selection of the next picture together with its accompanying sound is carried out by the control subsystem of the student's receiving set. If so, then it will be possible to serve an audience of a few thousand with a single program. On the other hand, it might turn out to be necessary, in order to make the program truly adaptive and responsive to the students, to use "feedback" channels from the students' homes to the narrowcasting stations. That would make it possible to transmit program material selected from a large store on a moment-to-moment basis and thereby to give each student a truly custom-made course, but it would limit the number of students that could be handled by a single transmission to a few hundred. When so few participants are to be accommodated, and when they all reside in the same area, it becomes likely that the best solution throughout the foreseeable future will be to bring the students together in one place and thereby simplify the communication problem. However, many technically competent people are unwilling to turn that statement of likelihood into a conclusion at this time, and more than a few think that, in fields that deal primarily with information, a modern version of "cottage industry" will prevail within a decade or two.

In any event, my hope is that enough channels will in due course become available to carry all the interactive power of computer-assisted teaching and learning into the home. Given enough channels, televised instructional systems — balanced systems in which the most highly interactive and the most dramatically dynamic techniques support and complement each other — will markedly improve the standard of education, the level of skill, and the quality of intellectual life in America.

INTERCOMMUNICATIONAL TELEVISION

From a point of view that is being taken by an increasing number of educators, "educational television" is perceived as the set of all the informational and communicational tools that can be fabricated out of wide-band channels. The prefix of "television" is taken literally, and the root is interpreted as meaning a large amount of communication channel capacity that should be put to the best possible use.

The applications of television envisaged from the viewpoint just described have to do more with communication within and among educational institutions than with communication between television stations and homes. It seems likely, therefore, that these applications will be developed sooner than applications based on similar techniques but requiring channels to receivers that are distributed throughout broad areas. Nevertheless, in the long term, there are clearly two parts to the idea of intercommunicational television. One of them focuses upon educational institutions — schools, colleges, universities, student bodies, faculties, laboratories, libraries, and so on. The other focuses upon community information centers and home information systems. In concept, the community information center is a projection and augmentation of the educational television station, and the home information system is a projection and augmentation of the television-radio-phonograph-tape-recorder console.

At the present time, intercommunicational television is hardly an actuality at all. It is a collection of rich and attractive images that form part of a concept that is developing in the minds of a growing number of people. Closed-circuit television is an important part of the concept, but by no means the essence of it. The essence is a comprehensive, flexible, interactive, multipurpose information network that includes large collections of information and advanced facilities for storing, processing, transmitting, and displaying it. The media are diverse but coordinated, television playing its role in concert with speech communication, facsimile communication, and communication with and among digital computers. Indeed, computer-processible data bases loom large in the overall concept of the information network of the future. It is appropriate that educational television is studying (e.g., in the EDUCOM Summer Study on Information Networks*) its place within the overall picture and its interrelations with the other media.

"Overall process" is more descriptive than "overall picture," for an educational information network would be an active, dynamic, ever-changing thing. It would deal with many different kinds of information, stored in many different places and flowing among many different kinds of communicators through many different media and channels. Education uses printed documents, video records, computer programs, data, drawings, graphs, diagrams, still pictures, moving pictures, sound recordings, and live person-to-person, person-to-group, and group-to-group communications. The communicators are students, teachers,

*EDUCOM is the Interuniversity Communications Council. The report of the Summer Study (1966) will be published by John Wiley and Sons, New York.

research workers, librarians, documentalists, computer programmers, programmed computers, administrators, and managers. The functional tools used in teaching and research include lectures, demonstrations, documentaries, computer-assisted instruction, computer-facilitated learning, computer-mediated research, information retrieval, selective dissemination of information, computer-aided design, computer-assisted experimentation, "reactive mathematics," and "teleconferences." "Reactive mathematics" is mathematical thinking "at the console" — the computer reacts by carrying out whatever operation one writes down just as soon as he has written it. "Teleconferences" are conferences in which the participants remain in their homes or offices yet, with the aid of teletype, telephone, and television, work together in close interaction.

Not all of the foregoing require wide-band communication, but all can take advantage of it. All are seen as components of a comprehensive information network that would serve the classroom, the study, the library, the laboratory, the conference room, and the convention hall in an integrated way, each component supporting others and being supported by them. The planning and design of such a network (or networks) are currently of great interest, and one of the main questions concerns the role to be played by television. For the long term, it seems clear that television and the narrower-band media should operate in synergy as complementary channels in a coherent system. For the short term, however, it is difficult to see how to bring together in a meaningful way the narrow-band facilities available from the telephone and telegraph companies, the wide-band facilities owned or leased by educational television organizations, and other wide-band channels (including satellite channels) available from common carriers. A small but important part of the overall problem is whether all the so-called "television satellite" channels will be reserved for broadcast television or whether some of them will be assigned for use in multi-media educational networks.

Looking up again at the broad horizons, we may sense that, although the resolution of problems such as those just

mentioned may have very significant near-term consequences, they are unlikely to determine the basic structure
of educational communication in the long term. The amount
of communication will increase. The faster media and the
media of higher capacity will grow in importance, both in
relative measure and in absolute measure. The various
media will be used in more coordinated ways. Information
will, more and more, be encoded for processing by computers. Computers will enter into more and more phases
of educational communication (and, indeed, into more and
more phases of everyday life). When people communicate
with each other, in teaching and learning or in dealing with
complex problems of almost any kind, they will not merely
transmit information back and forth; they will employ computers to transform and test the information and to relate
their present ideas and facts to those already recorded.
Communications between men and machines will constitute
an increasing fraction of the total. Many people will have
personal computer programs, "alter egos in the machine,"
to serve them as representatives and secretaries, and some
of the communications that now involve people will be
taken care of by those programs. Indeed, a large fraction
of all communications will be communications between
computers.

Most of the foregoing "prediction" is simply projection
into the future of what now exists and is familiar to many.
Nothing in the list of statements is beyond the range of
technical feasibility. The uncertainties are mainly uncertainties of time scale, and they stem mainly from difficulties
in predicting the interactions among economic, social, and
psychological factors. On the one hand are those who see
in modern informational technology a firm promise of making education not only universally available but universally
achievable and universally attractive. On the other hand
are those who hold that our rate of progress toward any
such goals is limited essentially not by any lack of material
resources or facilities, but by lack of basic understanding
of the educational process. The position of wisdom no doubt
lies somewhere between the polar extremes, but wherever

it lies, it calls for continual examination of the full range of possibilities offered by technology and periodic reassessment of our plans and courses of action in the light of those possibilities.

As a conclusion to this paper, let me presume to offer a tentative assessment. The main trend of educational television is somewhat too conservative in its estimation of the feasibility of selective, interactive, and intercommunicational television systems and of the achievability, with the aid of such systems, of a significant breakthrough in education. The main factor that is not sufficiently appreciated, I believe, is the effectiveness of interactive participation in a well-designed, strongly reinforcing educational process. Advances in technology are making it possible for the first time to set up such a process without depending upon lavish use of scarce human resources. Other advances are making it at least conceivable that we may be able to set up such processes on a broad enough scale to reach almost every educable member of the society. My conclusion, therefore, is that the situation calls for intensive research in two complementary fields: the exploitability of informational technology in support of education, and education within the new context offered by informational technology.

COMMERCIAL TELEVISION

by Hyman H. Goldin

Dr. Goldin is Executive Secretary, Carnegie Commission on Educational Television, and Associate Professor of Communications, Boston University.

A.B., Harvard College, 1936; M.A., 1946, Ph.D., 1951, Harvard University.

Staff Member of the Federal Communications Commission, 1943–1965; Chief, Economics Division, 1948–1961; Chief, Economics and Research Division, 1961–1963; Assistant Chief of the Broadcast Bureau, 1963–1965.

Television in the United States is predominantly commercial television. The channel carrying educational television into the home is only one of many: throughout the United States there are five commercial television stations for each educational station. In operating income the disparity is even greater: commercial television operates at a level in excess of $2 billion a year; educational television at about 3 percent of that amount. At any evening hour the commercial stations capture approximately ten times as many viewers; the commercial stations, moreover, are on the air before the educational day begins, and remain on long after the educational day has ended; commercial stations are on throughout the weekend when many educational stations are dark.

There are intimate and profound relationships between the two systems. The audience that educational television does command it owes, in a certain sense, to commercial television. The American people have invested more than $20 billion in television sets, and are currently purchasing sets at a rate of over $2 billion annually. With insignificant exceptions, those sets are purchased to provide access to commercial television. Commercial television, in that manner, has made it possible to bring the educational channel into the living room. The transmitters, the videotape recorders, the control-room electronics were all developed in response to the needs of commercial television, and are available to educational television at prices that would be exorbitantly higher if commercial television were not in the market.

Commercial television, too, has provided financial assistance. Networks and local systems have made grants in cash and capital equipment to educational stations and continue to do so; for example, in the years from 1961 to 1965, NBC gave $1,100,000, CBS $1,950,000, and ABC $250,000. Network programs not carried in some particular areas by the local network affiliate have at times been made available at no cost to the educational station. Such support represents both a generous sense of public service and an enlightened self-interest. The existence of an educational station in a television market, by its occupation of the channel, reduces commercial competition for advertising revenues, while its small audience does not in fact constitute real competition for viewers. The financial assistance from commercial television has been real, and in some cities (of which New York is the most noteworthy example) decisive in keeping the educational station on the air.

In one important aspect, the two systems have been almost entirely discrete: there is only a small flow of staff or talent across the boundary between them. Producers, directors, and writers, in whose hands lies the responsibility for creating television programs, tend to develop within one system or the other and to remain there. In educational television, especially in the stations licensed to educational institutions, recruitment takes place largely from within the field of education, and the television station takes on some of the characteristics of an audiovisual department in a school of education. There is a somewhat larger flow of technical staff, but it is usually from the low wage scales and limited opportunities of educational television to the richer fields of commercial television.

At first glance, the two systems have quite distinct functions. Yet there is considerable overlap between them. Both, for example, take advertising (although the educational system, under limitations imposed by Federal Communications Commission regulations, solicits in a most gingerly fashion, and calls the revenues underwriting). Both carry formal instruction (although on the schedules of the commercial networks it rarely appears after 7:00 A.M.). Both seek mass audiences, but the search is a matter of life or death only for the commercial system. Both offer programs for specialized audiences, the educational system as a basic character of its service, the commercial system for a variety of reasons.

Primarily, however, the commercial system has preempted three of the broadest areas within the field of communications. The first of these is advertising. The second is mass entertainment. The third is national and international news, upon which the networks spend much more money every year than is available to educational television for all purposes.

In each of those areas, commercial television has been impressively successful. Television is the dominant medium for national advertising. In 1965, network television billings were $338 million for ABC, $492 million for CBS, and $430 million for NBC. In the same year advertising revenues for *Life, Time,* and *Look* combined were $323 million. The statistics for mass entertainment are equally stupendous: for any practical purpose it is safe to think of almost every home in the United States as equipped with at least one television set; the average home has a television set in use from five to six hours daily; and audiences as large as 60 million for a single program are occasionally achieved. In the domain of news, surveys leave the impression that many people not only are more dependent upon television news than upon any other source but also tend to give it greater credence.

Figures like these have their special significance. They are achieved despite the criticisms of advertising on commercial television as often irritating and sometimes misleading and the criticisms of the news coverage as too limited

and lacking in depth. As for the system's performance in
the field of mass entertainment, it is under constant criticism. Most of the complaints can be summed up in charges
that television entertainment is pitched to a standard of
taste which is too low, that it is produced by formula and
frequently is trite and uninvolving, that it fails by its own
proclaimed standard of being somewhat ahead of popular
taste and in fact tends to deteriorate the standards of public taste. Yet, however valid the attacks and however per-
suasive one critic or another may find them, the hard fact
remains that the American people have turned to commercial television as they have never turned to any other mass
medium. American television of the sixties, like American
motion pictures of the thirties, moves across the face of the
globe except where powerful political forces establish barriers against it — and in some cases even despite those
barriers.

This very success has imposed certain constraints on
commercial television. Its great success has taken place in
a technical environment which television shares in part with
radio but with no other mass medium. There is room in the
electromagnetic spectrum for only a limited number of television stations, and it has been necessary to establish a governmental agency to preside over the assignment of those
stations. The assignments have been made with the public
interest in mind; in general, the intent has been to distribute
television stations equitably among the states and communities. In practice this distribution gives viewers in large
metropolitan centers a reasonably wide choice of channels;
viewers far removed from metropolitan centers have at least
one, and usually two or three. But the pattern of allocation
has had another consequence: the limited number of VHF
stations have had little or no effective competition and, as
a group, have been extremely profitable.

The development of UHF equipment and subsequent
legislation obliging set manufacturers to build all-channel
sets are slowly reducing the monopoly of VHF channel
owners. Wired television, if it becomes an independent
program service supported by advertising or subscription,

might ultimately alter the state of affairs far more significantly. Up to now, however, the method of channel assignment has been such that only two national networks could
be fully accommodated, with less than complete facilities
available to air the programs of the third network.

In such circumstances, the great monetary rewards come
from courting the mass audience, since that audience is not
yet saturated. In effect, the networks can sell all the evening time they have. The affiliates, deriving the bulk of
their revenues from the sale of non-network spot announcements, establish their rate cards on the basis of the audiences they reach and find moreover that sales come easier
as audiences grow larger. Thus the pressures at the station
and network levels are for larger and larger audiences.

Virtually all stations have local news and public affairs
programs and feature films. Most of the other programming
is delegated to the networks, for the networks have developed to an impressive degree the ability to attract mass
audiences. Prime time is given over largely to network
programs and the daytime hours, too, but the latter in
the form of either less costly programs (daytime audiences
are smaller and hence rates are necessarily lower) or filmed
reruns of previous prime-time programs. Into the late night
and the early morning hours network programs and movies
spread inexorably.

The struggle for audience at the networks is waged in
the context of an honest sense of institutional responsibility,
but is sometimes in conflict with it. That sense of responsibility may vary in degree among the networks, and may
vary with time at any one of the networks. To some extent,
however, it is always present. At the highest levels, there
is a recognition that the network cannot give over all of
its time to the search for the maximum audience; that it has
social and artistic responsibilities it cannot ignore. So NBC
presents its *White Papers;* CBS its *CBS Reports;* ABC its
Stage 67 — all fully aware that those programs will play to
small audiences.

The networks rarely recover the full costs of such programs, but the expected losses are a relatively minor deter-

rent. What is important is that the listing of such programs on a schedule may drive many viewers away for an entire evening. A viewer who tunes away from CBS at 7:30, when *CBS Reports* formerly was aired, may not return for the rest of the evening; having once engaged in the positive act of switching away from CBS, the viewer may not later engage in the positive act of switching back, and certainly the program adjacent to *CBS Reports* will suffer in audience ratings. Conversely, a viewer who is looking forward to *Bonanza* on NBC at 9 P.M. will tune his set to NBC at 8:00 or 8:30 and contentedly await his favorite. If the audience is to be maximized, an evening must be treated as a unit. Maximization of the audience is the business of commercial television.

The consequences are manifold. The price of failure can be so heavy that the network is reluctant to innovate if there is any other recourse. A successful program is imitated from network to network, and within the networks, until the wave dies out. Then some programming vice president is bold enough, and under enough pressures, to experiment with *Beverly Hillbillies* or *Batman*, and we have another relentless cycle during which those programs in turn are imitated.

Programming directed at something less than the mass audience is produced under tensions which often militate against quality. Should a network, for one reason or another, decide to present a series of serious dramas, the ratings are anxiously studied to determine the longevity and position in the schedule of the series; aside from an occasional special, serious drama has no established position in the television schedule as it has in almost every other country. A public affairs program or a news analysis sometimes will deteriorate as it passes through the various stages of production, because the producer is seeking desperately for some device to increase its rating. Whatever the intentions, and they are good more often than the critics of television customarily concede, they are carried out in an atmosphere which is not conducive to the soundest selection of quality programs and their best performance.

Those are harsh words, and should be qualified. The

record of the networks in news and public affairs is on the whole highly commendable. Even in entertainment, the superior program appears now and then, and if the quantity of such programming is small, it is small only in terms of television itself: counted in terms of hours per year, it is by no means insignificant.

In the end, however, commercial television remains true to its own purposes. It permits itself to be distracted as little as possible from its prime goal of maximizing audience. Only radical alterations in the entire system — and perhaps in our society itself — could alter its course. It is doing what it set out to do, and in its own terms successfully.

Meanwhile, by the wealth of its resources and the technical skill with which they are used, commercial television imposes constraints upon educational television. Clearly it can outbid educational television for talent. The outstanding writer would be worth as much to educational television as to commercial, but educational television cannot pay his price. What is quite as difficult for educational television, its more powerful neighbor establishes standards of performance and technique that educational television now finds impossible to meet. The television viewer is accustomed to the finesse of commercial television, and to its bottomless reservoir of human and technical resources. On production budgets that are a twentieth or a hundredth or a thousandth of those customary in commercial television, matching finesse cannot be provided nor the resources brought to bear. Educational television sometimes shows great skill in avoiding direct comparison with commercial television by going about its business skillfully and imaginatively in its own way. But there is a limit to such a process, and the hard fact remains that a documentary on educational television will be compared by its viewers with a documentary on commercial television. Whatever its superiority in substance, it cannot hope to match the commercial documentary in form or style or finesse.

It is most significant to any consideration of educational television to recognize the nature of the television world of which it is a part. Whatever its aspirations, and whatever may in the end be its accomplishments, educational television exists and will continue to exist in community with a commercial system that has most of the funds, most of the resources, and most of the viewers. That framework need not be restrictive — indeed, within such a framework, educational television, properly financed and properly directed, can find its greatest opportunities.

Educational television, and particularly Public Television, can serve as the mouthpiece and mirror of the local community. It will not be bound by the constraints of centralized network schedules, and it will have the incentive and resources to develop as a local institution in the best tradition of the local newspaper, the local theater, the local art gallery, and the local forum.

Most important, Public Television will have both the freedom and facilities to experiment, to innovate, to range over the whole spectrum of human interests. For Public Television, such an approach to programming will be neither exceptional nor special, but its norm. For those who complain that the daily fare of commercial television offers little real choice, for those who feel that television should enrich family experiences, Public Television should offer a welcome alternative.

The Federal Communications Commission and Educational Television Stations
by Hyman H. Goldin

Reservations

The Federal Communications Commission in 1952 set aside 242 station channels (assignments) for the exclusive use of noncommercial educational television. The assignments included 80 in the very high frequency (VHF) band and 162 in the ultra high frequency (UHF) band. As a general principle, a VHF channel was reserved in every community with three or more VHF assignments, unless the channels had already been licensed to commercial stations. In many large centers, including Chicago, Boston, Pittsburgh, San Francisco, St. Louis, Minneapolis, and Houston, the Federal Communications Commission reserved VHF channels for educational stations; in certain other major centers, however, where the VHF licenses had been granted earlier, such as Washington, New York, Los Angeles, Detroit, and Baltimore, the Commission reserved UHF channels. In addition a VHF reservation was made in forty-six educational centers having fewer than three VHF assignments.

Subsequently, by 1966, the Federal Communications Commission, acting on individual requests from educational organizations, increased the number of reservations to 329. In February 1966, the Commission issued an overall revision of its UHF assignment table for the nation: this new plan sets aside approximately 25 percent of the UHF reservations for education. Altogether, 623 reservations are specifically available to educational television in the United States (116 VHF and 507 UHF). In addition, petitions may be made to the Federal Communications Commission for additional reservations, and an educational organization may also apply to obtain a regular channel which is open both to commercial and noncommercial applicants. Approximately twelve such stations, including WNDT in the New York area, and WHYY, Wilmington, are operating as noncommercial educational stations on nonreserved channels.

Rules and Regulations

The Federal Communications Commission (FCC) Rules and Regulations contain certain provisions concerning the licensing and operation of noncommercial educational television stations.

The Rules state that "noncommercial educational broadcast stations will be licensed only to nonprofit educational organizations upon a showing that the proposed stations will be used primarily to serve the educational needs of the community; for the advancement of educational programs; and to furnish a nonprofit and noncommercial television broadcast service." Both public and private educational organizations qualify, and when determining their eligibility the FCC takes accreditation into consideration. Municipalities or other political subdivisions having no independently constituted educational organization which could apply are also eligible if they submit a showing that grant of the license will be consistent with the intent and purpose of the educational television service. In addition, community groups consisting of local public and private institutions, including educational institutions, may also be granted licenses upon the requisite showing. In practice, these licensing requirements have not posed any substantial difficulties for applicants. Unlike commercial television, there are no limitations on the number or location of noncommercial educational stations which can be licensed to a single entity.

In addition to supplying details concerning their legal qualifications, applicants must also furnish the FCC with information about the costs of constructing and operating their stations and how they plan to meet these costs, the nature of the programming to be presented, and details of the engineering aspects of the stations applied for.

Noncommercial educational television stations may transmit educational, cultural, and entertainment programs. The educational programs may be designed for use by educational institutions for in-school instruction, for teacher instruction, or for adult instruction. An educational station may receive financial support from educational institutions but it must not otherwise accept consideration for the broadcast of programs. It may use programs produced by or at the expense of or furnished by others, and it must, in those cases, make announcements to that effect, provided that no announcement promoting the sale of a product or service shall be transmitted in connection with any program.

In general, however, educational television stations are subject to the same operating, technical, and other requirements as commercial stations, including those with respect to treatment of controversial issues of public importance and political broadcasts.

Instructional Television Fixed Service

In 1964, the FCC established an "instructional television fixed service" in the 2500–2690 megacycle range "for the transmission of instructional, cultural, and other types of educational material to one or more fixed locations." This service has been used in large part by public and private educational organizations to transmit educational material to participating schools, colleges, and universities which are equipped with special elevated antennas to receive material. Because it is a point-to-point service, it is best suited to provide instructional programming to schools and other receiving points where sufficient viewers can be brought together to warrant the cost of the special receiving antennas, rather than to provide more general educational programming for the public. Relatively low-powered transmitters provide line-of-sight coverage to the special antennas installed at the various school buildings and other receiving points, but regular television receivers are used in the classrooms.

A single applicant may be authorized to use four channels to provide simultaneous programming to the schools and other receiving points to be served. In any metropolitan area there are theoretically thirty-one channels available for instructional television fixed station use, but these frequencies are shared with operational fixed and international control stations, some of which were authorized before the instructional television fixed service was established. The demand for these frequencies from educational users is growing and may result in full occupancy soon in a number of metropolitan areas.

Financial and Operating Reports of Educational Television Stations, July 1965–June 1966

(A Survey by the Commission)

TABLE 1
Educational Television Stations, 1965–1966

Number of stations on the air, June 1966	114
Total stations for which reports have been received [a]	113
By type of licensee:[b]	
Community [c]	41
School	19
State [d]	24
University	29

[a] The total number of reports received was 96; in several cases more than a single station was included in a report. The reports did not uniformly provide information on all schedules.

[b] The classification of stations by type of licensee is approximate only and used herein for statistical purposes.

[c] Includes WNYC–TV, licensed to New York City.

[d] Two states, Georgia and Alabama, provided information on more than one station in a single report (three in Georgia and six in Alabama) without breakdown of the operations of the separate stations which were linked in the state systems. The nine stations included are used in these tabulations as two stations.

TABLE 2

Educational Television Stations, 1965–1966

BROADCAST TIME

	All Stations	Community	School	State	University
Number of hours/week on the air					
Under 50	38	9	12	1	16
50 and over	57	25	6	13	13
Median	55	64	45	67	45
Number of days/week on the air					
5 or less	60	12	18	9	21
6	21	12	—	3	6
7	14	10	—	2	2
Number of weeks/year on the air					
40 or less	13	3	8	—	2
More than 40 but less than 52	7	2	—	1	4
52	75	29	10	13	23

TABLE 3

CURRENT YEAR EXPENDITURES [a]

Type of Station	Capital[b]	Station Operation	Total
All stations			
Total	$23,140,952	$34,340,994	$57,481,946[c]
Median	90,000	255,830	359,682
Community stations			
Total	7,594,282	17,461,014	25,055,296
Median	106,483	320,386	482,259
School stations			
Total	3,187,040	3,921,409	7,108,449
Median	30,054	208,689	300,000
State stations			
Total	7,728,441	6,483,727	14,212,168
Median	300,000	189,451	480,474
University stations			
Total	4,631,189	6,474,844	11,106,033
Median	68,800	186,000	331,600

---

[a] In the absence of a uniform system of accounts, the financial data are subject to reporting differences as among the stations. Particular problems exist where stations are part of larger organizations, such as university stations. Some of the costs of these stations and some of the funds may be allocated to other organizational units of the university.

[b] Sums expended or committed for capital outlays.

[c] Differences in cumulative totals in Tables 3, 5, 6, 10, and 11 are due to differences in the reporting of the individual stations, and failure to answer fully each schedule in the financial survey.

TABLE 4

DISTRIBUTION OF CURRENT YEAR EXPENDITURES, CAPITAL AND OPERATING

	All Stations	Community	School	State	University
Under $100,000	8	4	2	—	2
$100,000–250,000	19	5	5	3	6
$250,000–500,000	34	9	8	4	13
$500,000–750,000	12	3	1	2	6
$750,000–1,000,000	6	4	—	—	2
$1,000,000–1,500,000	5	4	—	1	—
$1,500,000–2,000,000	4	3	—	1	—
Over $2,000,000	5	2	1	2	—

TABLE 5

SOURCES OF CURRENT YEAR FUNDS

	All Stations Total	%	Community Total	%	School Total	%	State Total	%	University Total	%
Local Government	$11,057,597	18.9	$ 5,953,714	21.4	$4,127,545	88.4	$ 345,487	2.2	$ 630,851	6.0
State Government[a]	15,791,718	27.1	2,058,998	7.4	202,804	4.4	12,118,298	78.6	1,411,618	13.4
State University	6,559,972	11.2	600,900	2.2	103	—	35,000	0.3	5,923,969	56.6
Federal Government	6,834,520	11.8	2,215,694	8.0	240,062	5.1	2,739,653	17.7	1,639,111	15.7
Foundation	8,425,730	14.4	8,181,111	29.5	3,519	0.1	41,500	0.3	199,600	1.9
Underwriting	1,095,131	1.9	1,017,943	3.6	1,588	—	53,000	0.4	22,600	0.2
Business	2,052,418	3.5	1,772,750	6.4	84,368	1.8	35,200	0.2	160,100	1.5
Subscribers	3,217,166	5.5	3,137,646	11.3	7,970	0.1	30,050	0.2	41,500	0.4
Other Income	3,281,212	5.7	2,809,305	10.2	4,094	0.1	11,261	0.1	456,552	4.3
TOTAL	$58,315,464[b]	100%	$27,748,061	100%	$4,672,053	100%	$15,409,449	100%	$10,485,901	100%

a Other than university.
b See Note c to Table 3.

TABLE 6

CURRENT YEAR OPERATING EXPENSES[a] BY TYPES OF EXPENSE

Type of Expense	All Stations	Community	School	State	University
Technical:					
Total	$10,003,645	$ 4,751,299	$1,059,989	$2,164,850	$2,027,507
Median	74,646	94,923	62,360	90,279	66,000
Program:					
Total	12,309,240	6,967,714	1,886,066	1,019,491	2,435,969
Median	100,000	124,758	96,239	89,823	80,400
General and administrative:					
Total	10,155,714	5,406,300	1,179,294	1,794,702	1,775,418
Median	52,159	95,149	31,539	73,169	40,904
Total station expenses					
	$32,468,599[b]	$17,125,313	$4,125,349	$4,979,043	$6,238,894
Median	$ 258,510	$ 310,854	$ 211,763	$ 302,134	$ 186,000

---

[a] Exclusive of capital expenditures but including normal maintenance.
[b] Additional stations reporting "Total Station Expenses" without a breakdown by types of expenses bring this total to $34,924,473. See Note c to Table 3.

TABLE 7

SELECTED EXPENSE ITEMS

Type of Station	Wages and Salaries	Outside Program Expenses	Fund Raising and Promotion
All Stations			
Total	$17,362,252	$807,108	$1,704,086
% of total station expenses[a]	52.9	2.7	6.1
Community			
Total	8,563,273	302,070	1,521,262
% of total station expenses	49.3	2.1	9.0
School			
Total	2,747,867	129,043	16,850
% of total station expenses	66.6	3.2	1.1
State			
Total	2,261,592	108,877	50,439
% of total station expenses	45.4	2.5	1.2
University			
Total	3,789,520	267,118	115,535
% of total station expenses	59.6	4.2	2.2

[a] Percentages computed for those stations reporting specific items listed.

TABLE 8

NUMBER OF EMPLOYEES

Type of Station	Full-Time	Part-Time	Total Employees
All Stations			
Total	2,763	1,147	3,910
Median	23	8	31
Community			
Total	1,364	354	1,718
Median	25	7	34
School			
Total	397	115	512
Median	22	4	24
State			
Total	464	116	580
Median	24	5	30
University			
Total	538	562	1,100
Median	19	17	36

TABLE 9a

ANNUAL SALARIES OF SELECTED PERSONNEL CATEGORIES, BY TYPES OF STATIONS
All Stations

Personnel Categories	$5,000–7,500	7,500–10,000	10,000–15,000	15,000–20,000	Over 20,000
General Manager	—	3	49	28	8
Program Manager or Director	6	31	33	5	2
Production Manager or Director	14	35	15	3	—
Producer-Director, Senior	42	54	5	1	—
Chief Engineer	4	37	43	6	1
Public Relations Director	28	15	9	2	—
Special Project Director	5	11	11	4	1
Director of In-School Service	4	6	24	3	—

TABLE 9b

ANNUAL SALARIES OF SELECTED PERSONNEL CATEGORIES, BY TYPES OF STATIONS
Community Stations

Personnel Categories	$5,000–7,500	7,500–10,000	10,000–15,000	15,000–20,000	Over 20,000
General Manager	—	—	10	14	8
Program Manager or Director	2	8	13	5	2
Production Manager or Director	4	13	6	3	—
Producer-Director, Senior	9	17	5	1	—
Chief Engineer	—	9	16	6	1
Public Relations Director	9	5	8	2	—
Special Project Director	1	4	8	3	1
Director of In-School Service	2	1	14	1	—

TABLE 9c

ANNUAL SALARIES OF SELECTED PERSONNEL CATEGORIES, BY TYPES OF STATIONS
School Stations

Personnel Categories	$5,000–7,500	7,500–10,000	10,000–15,000	15,000–20,000	Over 20,000
General Manager	—	2	12	1	—
Program Manager or Director	2	5	5	—	—
Production Manager or Director	5	6	2	—	—
Producer-Director, Senior	8	7	—	—	—
Chief Engineer	2	7	8	—	—
Public Relations Director	2	1	—	—	—
Special Project Director	—	1	—	—	—
Director of In-School Service	—	1	1	2	—

TABLE 9d

ANNUAL SALARIES OF SELECTED PERSONNEL CATEGORIES, BY TYPES OF STATIONS
State Stations

Personnel Categories	$5,000–7,500	7,500–10,000	10,000–15,000	15,000–20,000	Over 20,000
General Manager	—	—	8	4	—
Program Manager or Director	—	3	6	—	—
Production Manager or Director	2	5	—	—	—
Producer-Director, Senior	10	7	—	—	—
Chief Engineer	1	7	5	—	—
Public Relations Director	6	4	1	—	—
Special Project Director	—	3	2	—	—
Director of In-School Service	—	2	2	—	—

TABLE 9e

ANNUAL SALARIES OF SELECTED PERSONNEL CATEGORIES, BY TYPES OF STATIONS

University Stations

Personnel Categories	$5,000–7,500	7,500–10,000	10,000–15,000	15,000–20,000	Over 20,000
General Manager	—	1	19	9	—
Program Manager or Director	2	15	9	—	—
Production Manager or Director	3	11	7	—	—
Producer-Director, Senior	15	23	—	—	—
Chief Engineer	1	14	14	—	—
Public Relations Director	11	5	—	—	—
Special Project Director	4	3	1	1	—
Director of In-School Service	2	2	7	—	—

TABLE 10

CUMULATIVE HISTORICAL STATION COSTS SINCE INCEPTION

Type of Station	Total Capital Costs	Total Operating Costs	All Costs
All Stations	$83,591,203	$169,090,280	$252,681,479 [a]
Community	36,978,721	85,525,293	122,504,010
School	9,335,066	19,769,390	29,104,456
State	16,628,289	29,801,979	46,430,268
University	20,649,127	33,993,618	54,642,745

[a] See Note c to Table 3.

TABLE 11

CUMULATIVE HISTORICAL SOURCES OF FINANCIAL SUPPORT SINCE INCEPTION

	All Stations Total	%	Community Total	%	School Total	%	State Total	%	University Total	%
Local Government	$ 58,267,938	23.2	$ 29,330,126	24.1	$24,486,965	83.5	$ 636,830	1.4	$ 3,814,017	6.9
State Government[a]	55,888,822	22.3	5,385,199	4.4	1,086,508	3.7	38,457,420	85.9	10,959,695	19.9
State University	27,670,825	11.0	1,215,269	1.0	25,906	0.1	1,134,526	2.6	25,295,124	45.8
Federal Government	13,145,625	5.2	6,178,767	5.1	888,967	3.0	2,721,719	6.0	3,356,172	6.1
Foundation	33,711,563	13.4	26,371,894	21.6	1,350,161	4.6	452,508	1.0	5,537,000	10.0
Subscribers	21,567,179	8.6	20,271,124	16.7	133,510	0.4	53,975	0.1	1,108,570	2.0
Program Grants	10,293,106	4.1	9,388,816	7.7	469,272	1.6	75,000	0.2	360,018	0.7
Underwriting	3,478,688	1.4	2,812,127	2.3	238,761	0.9	189,400	0.4	238,400	0.4
Business	16,888,528	6.7	14,751,720	12.1	351,500	1.2	1,052,708	2.4	732,600	1.3
Other Income	10,295,007	4.1	6,170,895	5.0	320,206	1.0	20,836	—	3,783,070	6.9
TOTAL	$251,207,281[b]	100%	$121,875,937	100%	$29,351,756	100%	$44,794,922	100%	$55,184,666	100%

a Other than university.
b See Note c to Table 3.

Estimates of Educational Television
Audiences, 1965, 1966

TABLE 1

ESTIMATES OF ETV AUDIENCE, OCTOBER 1966
(A. C. Nielsen Company)

U.S. total homes	58,243,800
U.S. television homes	54,921,970
Number of homes tuning to one or more ETV stations in average week	6,860,000 [a]
Percent of homes tuning to one or more ETV stations in average week	12.5 percent
Average hours of viewing of ETV per home per week	1.2 hours/week
Number of hours of viewing of ETV stations per week	8,240,000

[a] Assuming 2.4 viewers per viewing home, the total number of persons reached by all ETV stations in a week exceeds 16,000,000.

TABLE 2

ESTIMATES OF ETV AUDIENCE, 1965
(American Research Bureau)

U.S. total homes	57,810,700
U.S. television homes	54,456,300
Net weekly circulation of ETV stations (homes)	4,883,900
ETV share of net weekly circulation	9.0 percent
Total hours spent viewing ETV stations	6,771,600
Average family who watches ETV at least once per week views ETV	1.4 hours/week

TABLE 3

LARGEST 30 EDUCATIONAL TELEVISION STATIONS BY NET WEEKLY AND AVERAGE DAILY CIRCULATION, MARCH 1966

(American Research Bureau)

Television Market	Call Letters	Net Weekly Circulation[a] Homes	Rank	Ave. Daily Circulation[b] Homes	Rank
New York	WNDT	1,855,700	1	496,000	1
Boston	WGBH	335,800	2	74,100	2
San Francisco	KQED	290,800	3	70,500	3
Chicago	WTTW	277,300	4	57,100	7
Wilmington–Philadelphia	WHYY	274,400	5	65,700	5
Los Angeles	KCET	202,200	6	61,500	6
Pittsburgh	WQED	260,400	7	65,800	4
Milwaukee	WMVS	117,300	8	29,500	8
Miami	WTHS	109,800	9	26,300	9
Denver	KRMA	98,500	10	24,500	10
St. Louis	KETC	91,300	11	17,300	12
Seattle	KCTS	83,800	12	20,100	11
Houston	KUHT	67,400	13	13,700	18

Portland, Oregon	KOAP	66,000	14	15,400	13
Hartford	WEDH	61,200	15	14,500	16
Sacramento	KVIE	58,800	16	14,900	15
Tampa–St. Petersburg	WEDU	54,900	17	14,200	17
Washington, D.C.	WETA	53,200	18	15,000	14
Minneapolis–St. Paul	KTCA	52,600	19	10,700	21
Athens, Ga.	WGTV	46,900	20	11,300	20
San Antonio–Austin	KLRN	46,900	21	11,500	19
Salt Lake City	KUED	39,400	22	8,200	24
New Orleans	WYES	39,300	23	8,000	25
Lincoln	KUON	36,800	24	9,000	23
Chapel Hill	WUNC	34,900	25	7,900	26
Detroit	WTVS	34,800	26	7,700	27
Dallas	KERA	34,800	27	7,500	28
Albuquerque	KNME	31,700	28	9,400	22
Durham	WENH	26,700	29	5,800	30
Memphis	WKNO	26,700	30	5,700	29

a NET Weekly Circulation—The estimated number of different television homes viewing a particular station at least once per week, Monday-Sunday, 6:00 a.m.-2:00 a.m., EST. ARB circulation data comes directly from recorded evidence of viewing in ARB diaries.

b Average Daily Circulation—The estimated average number of different television homes reached by a particular station on each day of the week, Monday-Sunday, 6:00 a.m.–2:00 a.m., EST.

TABLE 4

COMPOSITION OF ETV AUDIENCE

(Institute for Communication Research, Stanford University)

Proportions of the WQED, Pittsburgh, and WGBH, Boston, monthly audience representing different educational and occupational groups, March 1966.

Education	Pittsburgh	Boston
8th grade or less	5.8%	3.4%
Some high school	11.3%	6.4%
Completed high school	33.1%	40.4%
Some college	16.5%	18.8%
Completed college	21.4%	21.5%
Study beyond A.B.	11.9%	9.5%
(Interview base, 2,051)		

Occupation	Pittsburgh	Boston
Professional	17.2%	14.6%
Business, gov't.	22.3%	24.0%
Clerical	10.7%	10.9%
Technicians, skilled labor	16.2%	19.6%
Unskilled labor	20.9%	11.9%
Students	1.0%	4.4%
Housewives	1.8%	5.9%
Retired	9.9%	8.7%
(Interview base, 2,003)		